Jasper National Park

Behind the Mountains and Glaciers

David M. Baird

Hurtig Publishers, Edmonton
in co-operation with
Parks Canada
and the
Geological Survey of Canada

Revised edition
Copyright © Minister of Supply and Services Canada 1977

Hurtig Publishers
10560 105 Street
Edmonton, Alberta

Co-published through
Publishing Centre
Supply and Services Canada
Catalogue No. R61-2/6-1

ISBN 0-88830-130-8 cloth
ISBN 0-88830-131-6 paper

Photographs: David M. Baird
Maps and diagrams: Geological Survey of Canada
Design: David Shaw & Associates Ltd.

Printed and bound in Canada
by T.H. Best Printing Company Limited

Contents

How to use this book

If you haven't the time immediately to read it from the beginning, look at the illustrations and turn to the map facing page 64 to find the numbers of the stops along the route you are travelling. Then turn to the roadlogs (starting on page 81) and follow each stop carefully, for you will find that the beauty of the scene is increased for the traveller who knows something of what he is looking at and how it originated.

The first part of this guidebook describes in some detail the general aspects of the geology of Jasper National Park—where it is, how the mountains there originated, what the rocks of the region are and where they came from, and the different shapes of mountains related to the structures of the rocks composing them. This general background is followed by detailed descriptions of selected localities of special geological interest. The last part comprises a series of notes on what is to be seen at each of the lookouts and roadside stops along the main travel routes, with an index map to show where they are.

Most of the words used in a technical sense or which have an unusual meaning are italicized and are explained carefully where they are first used. If, however, you do not immediately find the meaning of a word, look in the index, for many of the unusual ones are listed there along with all place names and a great variety of subjects.

Although all measurements are given in metric units, the imperial equivalents have been added where it is felt they will be helpful. All distances between roadside stops are given in miles as well as kilometres.

Introduction

Jasper National Park is an area of superb scenery, stretching for 209 kilometres along the eastern slope of the Rocky Mountains from their western spine, along the British Columbia-Alberta boundary, eastward to the foothills. Its size, some 10,878 square kilometres (4,200 square miles), makes it one of the largest national parks in the world; and its location, astride the parallel ranges of the Rocky Mountain System, makes it one of the most beautiful.

The mountain ranges along the northeastern boundary of the park are cut into rocks of great complexity of structure so that individual peaks commonly show sweeping folds and great fractures. Mountains along the park's central ribs are cut into uplifted masses of horizontal or gently folded sedimentary rocks so that individual peaks are commonly clearly made up of flat or gently dipping layers. Amid the mountains lie beautiful alpine valleys with rushing streams and sparkling lakes.

The mountains in Jasper National Park are high enough to support numerous icefields and glaciers. The Columbia Icefield, an icecap covering many square kilometres, extends into the southern tip of the park and sends tongues of glacial ice down into the valleys there. All along the western edge of the park, the peaks and plateaus that rise more than 2,000 metres above sea level carry patches of permanent snow and small glaciers or icecaps; in many other places local glaciers add their beauty to the mountain scenery.

Erosion by glaciers in former times when they were more extensive has produced steep-walled valleys and great cliffs. Rivers have cut into the complex of folded and faulted rocks beneath the surface and made a variety of chasms, canyons, and valleys, and in some places form spectacular waterfalls where they tumble over ready-made cliffs. In one area the drainage disappears underground at several places to reappear kilometres away, having flowed through a system of tunnels, caves, and underground river channels cut in soluble limestones.

In the rocks themselves is written a history of ancient seas spreading over the land, and of thousands of metres of sand, silt, and gravel being deposited in the shallow marine waters that covered an area now occupied by snow-capped mountains. In the ancient seas, marine creatures lived and died; and their remains, in the form of imprints, or their shells and hard parts, are found as fossils in the rocks today.

Thus, for people who have time to look around carefully, Jasper National Park has a great array of wonderful scenery and many features of geological interest in the rocks into which the scenery is carved. Visitors who are impressed by the beauty of the scene, will find it even more moving when they reflect on the intricately woven patterns of events that have, through the millions of years, produced the rocks and the mountains, the rivers and the glaciers.

It is the purpose of this book to tell you something of all these things—the beauty, the formation of the scenery, and the history written in the rocks. But first let us examine the boundaries of the park to see exactly where it is; and, because many of the boundaries are divides, we should find out what divides really are.

Divides

As you travel up any river, you can see that it gets smaller above each of the tributaries that pours water into it from the sides. Thus, even the largest rivers rise in a multitude of very small streams which make up the bulk of the main river by uniting their waters. If you travel farther and farther up a small stream you will eventually come to where it begins as a tiny trickle of water. Such a place is usually near the top of a hill, for as rain falls on the hill it will naturally flow down the slopes on all sides. Thus, the crest of a ridge forms a natural divide between waters that flow down one side and waters that flow down the other. This is why, on the ground or on a map, a line drawn to separate two drainage systems is called a *divide.*

A look at a map of the whole of North America will quickly show you that some very large rivers flow into each of the oceans bordering this continent. If you were to follow these rivers to their very headwaters you should find a line separating the drainage to the Pacific Ocean from the drainage to the Atlantic Ocean, and other lines which divide Atlantic drainage from Arctic drainage and Arctic drainage from Pacific drainage. Thus the term *continental divide* is applied to the imaginary line that separates the drainage basins of a continent.

Ever since man first began to separate territories it has been convenient to divide them on the basis of drainage basins of rivers. Boundaries of countries, provinces, or even counties have commonly been defined as the divide between the water flowing to one side and water flowing to another. One such boundary is between the Province of Alberta and the Province of British Columbia. This divide, which runs right up the spine of the Rocky Mountains, separates waters that eventually end up in the rivers to the Pacific Ocean from those that will flow finally into the Atlantic Ocean. It is this same Continental Divide that forms the western boundary of Jasper National Park for 240 kilometres along the spine of the Rockies.

In North America, where drainage is split among three oceans, there is one place—in the icefield where Banff National Park and Jasper National Park come together—from which the drainage flows in three directions. Here, a single drop of rain or a single crystal of snow may split into parts that end up in the Arctic, Atlantic, and Pacific Oceans after flowing for thousands of kilometres in completely different river systems.

Boundaries of the Park

Jasper National Park comprises all of the land drained by the Athabasca River and its tributaries above the western end of Brûlé Lake, in addition to a large area drained by the Brazeau River in the southeastern corner and a smaller area drained by the Smoky River in the extreme northwestern corner. The park lies wholly within the Province of Alberta. Banff National Park, also in Alberta, adjoins it to the south. Jasper Park is bounded on its western side, along the Continental Divide, by Hamber Provincial Park in the south and by Mount Robson Provincial Park farther north, both in British Columbia.

The western boundary of Jasper Park follows the Continental Divide. From its junction with the boundary of Banff National Park, northwestward to a point about opposite Athabasca Falls, the divide separates the watershed of the Athabasca River, which drains eventually to the Arctic Ocean, from that of the Columbia River, which ends in the Pacific Ocean between Washington and Oregon. North of this point, the divide separates the watershed of the Athabasca River from that of the Fraser River, which empties into the Pacific Ocean at Vancouver. At the northwestern end of the park, the divide separates the Fraser River drainage from that of the Smoky River, which flows northward to join the Peace River and thence, via the Mackenzie River, flows into the Arctic Ocean.

The boundary between Jasper and Banff national parks is another divide, this one between the headwaters of the Sunwapta River, a tributary of the Athabasca River, and the headwaters of the North Saskatchewan River, which flows into Hudson Bay. At the Snow Dome, high in the Columbia Icefield, the park boundaries of Banff, Jasper, and Hamber all come together at one point. This is where waters of the Athabasca River flow north to the Arctic Ocean via the Mackenzie river system; where waters of the North Saskatchewan River flow southeastward then eastward to Hudson Bay and the Atlantic Ocean; and where Columbia River waters flow southwestward to empty eventually into the Pacific Ocean.

From where the Banff and Jasper park boundaries start to sepa-

8

Snow-covered Mount Robson looms majestically behind Lake Catherine. At 3,954 metres (12,972 feet), it is the highest peak in the Canadian Rockies. It lies in British Columbia, just to the west of the Continental Divide.

rate at the southeast corner, the Jasper park boundary follows an artificial line that makes a strange little bulb. The boundary then runs parallel to, but just southeast of the Brazeau River, from the river's source to its junction with a tributary from Brazeau Lake. It continues northeastward along the Brazeau River to the junction with the Southesk River, then back along the Southesk for about six kilometres. The long northeast boundary of Jasper National Park follows a series of divides northeasterly to the park gate below Roche à Perdrix. Beyond that, it crosses the Athabasca River. From there, the boundary follows another series of divides in irregular steps all the way to its crossing of the Smoky River and beyond to Mount Lucifer at the northwest corner of the park.

You may wonder why the park has such irregular boundaries. The explanation is simple enough when you realize that these boundaries are based largely on divides. Divides make reasonable boundaries because the division of the waters is easily observed. Furthermore, divides make natural boundaries for national parks, which are game preserves as well as places of scenic beauty.

Origin of the Mountains

The surface of the earth has mountains of many different kinds: some stand as isolated masses whereas others occur in groups clearly related to one another; some tower thousands of metres above their surroundings whereas others (called "mountains" by the people who live there) may be only a hundred metres high. The wide variety of mountains points to a wide variety of origins.

In some parts of the world great masses of liquid lava and ash pour up from the depths of the earth to accumulate around volcanic vents. These are *volcanic mountains*. In other places, rivers and streams have cut deeply into high plateau areas over long periods of time to leave rough, mountainous terrain. In still other parts of the world, huge wrinklings in the earth's crust are made by tremendous compressive forces, in the same way that you can wrinkle the carpet on a floor by pushing against it with your foot. These make *folded mountains*. Another type of mountain results in places where the earth seems to have split along enormous faults or breaks and one of the sides may be uplifted thousands of metres. These are *fault-block mountains*.

When, however, we come to the great ranges of mountains—groups of clearly related mountains that extend for hundreds or even thousands of kilometres over the surface of the earth—we find a much more complicated story. One of the most interesting parts of this story is that the major mountain systems all over the world seem to have the same kind of history, with at least several chapters in

10

The great accumulation of snow on the northeast side of Mount Robson and adjacent peaks give rise to Robson Glacier, seen here from the northwest. Most of the area in view is in Mount Robson Provincial Park.

common. We call this type *geosynclinal mountains,* and it will help to know something about how they originate, for the mountains in the western Canadian national parks are of this kind.

To begin the story of these mountains we must go back into geological time about 1,000 million years. North America then was very different from the land we know today. Where we now find the Rocky Mountain System from the Arctic Ocean to Mexico, there existed a great flat area which was very close to sea level. Great forces in the interior of the earth caused the whole area to sink very slowly below sea level. The rate of this depression was probably only a few

A great anticline, or upfold, shows clearly in these limestone rocks in a tributary to Rocky River, seen in the distant valley.

centimetres in a thousand years but it continued over a very long period. It meant that the sea eventually flooded the land over hundreds of thousands of square kilometres from the Arctic Ocean to the Gulf of Mexico. Into this vast shallow inland sea the rivers from the surrounding regions poured their loads of silt and mud, which spread evenly over the bottom. Waves along the shores of these ancient seas eroded the land, added more sediments, and made currents to distribute them over the bottom, far from land.

As the millions of years passed, the accumulation of sedimentary materials—the mud, silt, and sand from the rivers and shorelines, and limy precipitates from the sea itself—gradually filled the shallow inland sea. At times, vast areas must have become filled up to near sea level. But one of the strange things about these great depressions in the earth's surface is the way they seem to have continued to sink as the load of sedimentary material in their centres increased. By this gradual sinking and an almost equal rate of filling it was possible for thousands and thousands of metres of sand, silt, and mud to accumulate, layer upon layer, and all show features of shallow-water origin.

At a time in the earth's history which geologists place at between 600 million and 500 million years ago, living things began to populate some parts of the seas fairly thickly. Some of these creatures had hard skeletons or outer coverings, and when they died these hard parts fell to the bottom and were promptly buried by the accumulating muds and silts.

In some places the hard parts of the dead animals made clear impressions on the sedimentary materials on the sea bottom. When the soft sedimentary materials hardened into solid rock (over a period of millions of years), the remains of the long-dead organisms became *fossils*.

How do we know these things took place where we now find the western mountains? We read it in the rocks where the story is fairly clearly written. The rocks of which the mountains are made are distinctly of sedimentary origin—that is, they are made of ancient gravels, sands, muds and various sediments that have become hardened into solid rock. They are layered or *stratified* as we would expect accumulating sediments to be, because from time to time there were changes in the composition of the material being laid down.

These changes may have been due to storms, changes in wave patterns, changes in drainage systems, or the changes that would take place as the land supplying the sediment was gradually being eroded away. On some of the rock surfaces we find ripple marks which are exactly like those found today in stream bottoms or in the shallow parts of the sea. By splitting open the rocks we can find the fossilized remains of ancient sea creatures, some of them with modern counterparts. Other fossilized skeletons are from creatures that have been extinct for millions of years, yet we can tell a great deal about them by comparing their structures with those of living creatures and noting carefully their association with creatures we know something about.

The kinds of materials the rocks are made of and all the structures found in them can be observed today in different parts of the world in the actual process of formation. We can estimate the extent of the ancient seas by looking for the rocks that were deposited in them. We can tell something of the existence of former shorelines by looking for evidence of beach deposits in the rocks. We can tell whether rocks were laid down as sediments in deep water or in shallow water by comparing what we find in the rocks with what we see being deposited in those environments now.

As to the development of the Rocky Mountains, we can conclude, by observing evidence of erosion still preserved in the rock record, that the seas withdrew temporarily from the region or that the sediments completely filled the shallow depression on the top of the continent. In short, by putting together and correlating hundreds of small pieces of scattered evidence, we can unravel with some certainty the story of the rocks from which the mountains were later carved.

The next chapter in the history of the Rocky Mountains seems to have begun about 200 million years ago. The rock record tells us that a disturbance of the very shallow depression on the surface of western North America, which, as we have observed above, became filled with sedimentary materials, began to change the pattern of development. Some areas of the old trough were lifted up out of the sea and were themselves eroded to supply sediments that were poured back into the remaining sea.

As the tens of millions of years passed, the crust of the earth apparently became more and more unstable in the region of what we now call the Rocky Mountains. This unrest culminated about 75 million years ago in a complete change. From the Arctic Ocean to the Gulf of Mexico the great thickness of rocks which had been accumulating as sediments on the old sea bottom in the previous billion years, was lifted above sea level, broken in many places along great fractures called *faults,* and in some places strongly compressed. The compression or squeezing caused the great blanket of rocks to fold and buckle, and in places to break so that one part slid up over another part. The forces within the earth that would cause this kind of uplift and breaking are so vast that it is difficult to comprehend them at all. Yet we can go to the mountains and once again clearly see proof of this chapter in the development of the Rocky Mountain System.

In very old mountain systems of the world, where long-continued erosion has cut into the very core of the mountains themselves, we can often observe in some detail a third chapter in the development of geosynclinal mountains. It seems that during or just after the folding and faulting, great masses of hot molten rock appear in the cores of mountain systems. These push rocks aside or melt their way into the interiors of the belts of folded and broken sedimentary rock, where they cool down and eventually solidify. Canada's Rocky Mountains have not been deeply enough eroded so we know nothing of this part of their history.

The next phase in the development of all geosynclinal mountain systems seems to be one of quiet stability, during which the agents of erosion—glaciers, rivers, and wind—contrive to cut deeply into the uplifted, complicated mass of broken and folded rocks. For some 70 million years now this has been the history of the Rocky Mountains in Canada.

For a very long time, scientists wondered why mountains occur where they do and why this kind of a history has taken place where it has. Now, within the decade of the sixties and the early seventies, a realization that the outer sections of the earth behave like enormous plates moving about on a mobile substrate, has suddenly made possible an understanding of many of the puzzles concerning the origin of major features of the earth's structure.

From a variety of lines of evidence, it is clear now that inner parts of the earth are plastic under the enormous pressures and elevated temperatures prevailing there. It seems, too, that currents moving infinitely slowly are generated in this plastic layer by the earth's inner heat sources. We all know that the outside of the earth, the part we

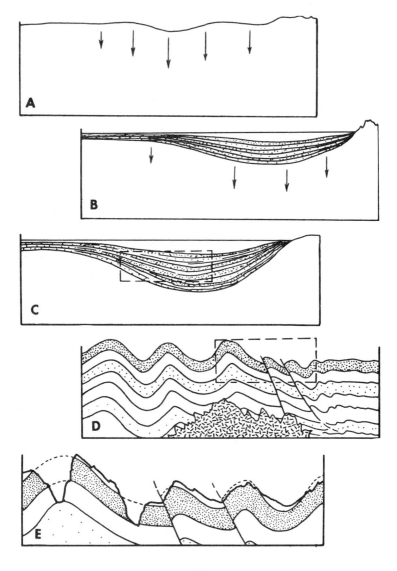

Development of Geosynclinal Mountains

The spectacular peaks and valleys of the Rocky Mountains as we know them today are made of rocks which record a story that began more than 600 million years ago. At that time part of western North America began to warp downward to form an elongated trough as in A.

Rivers poured sand, silt, and gravel into the lowland area. Downwarping continued until the trough was filled with a shallow sea, into which poured a steady flow of sedimentary materials, as in B.

Downsinking continued, but it seems to have been at a rate that corresponded closely to the rate of filling, so that sedimentation was always into shallow marine waters. The mass of sedimentary materials slowly changed to sedimentary rock as the load on top increased until it had a form like that in C.

For reasons we do not yet understand, the trough area was then severely compressed so that the rocks in it were folded and broken. At about this time in the history of such mountains great masses of molten materials commonly appear in the cores of the folded and broken rock, eventually solidifying into granite. D is what an enlarged section of C would look like.

Uplift accompanied the folding and faulting, and as soon as the rocks emerged from the sea they were subjected to erosion. Rivers and glaciers carved the valleys and formed the peaks as shown in E, an enlarged part of D. This is the stage of development of our Rocky Mountains now.

run around on, is solid; and it is thus conceived that sections of the outer solid part are moved about by the drag of the currents on their undersides. Thus, like ice cakes in a river in spring, enormous sectors of the earth's solid layer move against one another, bumping and scraping, riding over and under one another, on a scale that deals with whole continents and ocean basins in size, and in time in millions upon millions of years to move a few hundreds of metres.

The real cause of mountains lies in this motion of the earth's great plates. Look at the Rockies, and try to imagine that the whole of North America is being thrust westwards against a great block of the earth's crust under the floor of the Pacific Ocean and merely

The Front Ranges of the Rocky Mountains provide spectacular views of fold and fault structures in some of the cross valleys. Here, upfolds and downfolds are visible in the north wall of one of the main tributaries of Alpland Creek, about thirteen kilometres east of the upper end of Medicine Lake.

wrinkling the edges. All the rest follows from this grand concept.

At the present time, as we drive through the river valleys and among the mountain peaks, we can observe erosion as it proceeds. We can actually watch the glaciers pushing and scraping over the country, tearing off rock and grinding it up, some of it as fine as flour. We can see the rivers cutting into their rocky courses, wearing away the land, and carrying their loads of debris towards the ocean. We can observe great masses of gravel, sand, and silt—the results of erosion of mighty mountains through tens of thousands of years—now spread out below the foot of the mountains. Erosion has cut valleys deep into the complicated rock structures to reveal much of the story of folding, faulting and uplift.

Let us next see what rocks were laid down in the ancient seaway that covered Jasper National Park so that we can appreciate what makes the bulk of the mountains there now.

The Rocks

If we could find a place where all the rocks of any section of the park are exposed in one huge cliff, or if we could bore a hole down through the complete section of rocks and take samples, it would be possible at one place to compile a geological column. In most areas, however, evidence of the succession of rocks is compiled from many sites where different parts of the rock section are exposed. In these columns it is customary to place the youngest rocks on top and the oldest rocks on the bottom. This follows the *law of superposition* which says, simply, that if a series of rock layers were laid down, one on top of another, the youngest or most recent layer would be on top and the oldest or first layer would be on the bottom. Thus, when we look at a mountain, the youngest rocks are those in the tops of the peaks and the oldest are those on the bottom. This relationship is disturbed by extremes of folding or faulting where the whole rock sequence is actually turned over or where older rocks are bodily thrust up on top of younger rocks; but this is a rare condition.

The rocks of Jasper National Park include a wide range of types and represent a long span of geological time. The oldest are classed as *Precambrian,* that is, they were laid down in that vast expanse of time between the beginning of the earth and a point in time about 550 million years ago. The youngest solid rocks are classed as *Cretaceous,* that is, they were laid down in a period of geological time that spanned about 50 million years, ending about 65 million years ago. Because of the structure of the rocks and the manner of their erosion, the youngest rocks are exposed in the eastern section of the park and the oldest are exposed in the mountains and valleys of the western section. It is thus convenient to divide the description of these rocks into two sections. One section includes the parts visible from the Banff-Jasper road, from the southern boundary of the park to Jasper townsite and the Jasper-Yellowhead highway; the other deals with the area seen along the Jasper-Edmonton road from Jasper to the eastern gate.

These glaciers and snowfields lie on the east slope of Calumet Peak, in the northwest of Jasper National Park, west of the trail along Snake Indian Pass.

Banff—Jasper—Yellowhead

In the mountains of Jasper National Park we would expect to find the oldest rocks in places that have been uplifted and then deeply eroded. In any one mountainside we would look for them in the bottoms of the cliffs and in the valleys. It happens that the structure and history of erosion in the Rocky Mountains in the region of Jasper National Park brings the oldest rocks to the surface along the western and west-central areas of the park. The long valley systems of the Bow River, the headwaters of the North Saskatchewan, and the Sunwapta-Athabasca river systems are all cut into very old rocks, with

21

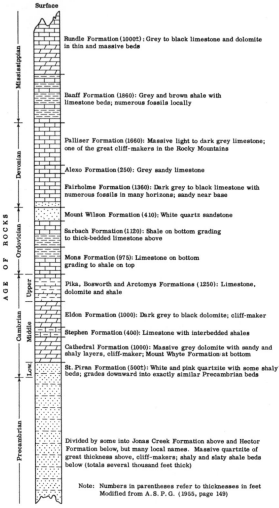

Rundle Formation (1000±): Grey to black limestone and dolomite in thin and massive beds

Banff Formation (1860): Grey and brown shale with limestone beds; numerous fossils locally

Palliser Formation (1660): Massive light to dark grey limestone; one of the great cliff-makers in the Rocky Mountains

Alexo Formation (250): Grey sandy limestone

Fairholme Formation (1360): Dark grey to black limestone with numerous fossils in many horizons; sandy near base

Mount Wilson Formation (410): White quartz sandstone

Sarbach Formation (1120): Shale on bottom grading to thick-bedded limestone above

Mons Formation (975): Limestone on bottom grading to shale on top

Pika, Bosworth and Arctomys Formations (1250): Limestone, dolomite and shale

Eldon Formation (1000): Dark grey to black dolomite; cliff-maker

Stephen Formation (400): Limestone with interbedded shales

Cathedral Formation (1000): Massive grey dolomite with sandy and shaly layers, cliff-maker; Mount Whyte Formation at bottom

St. Piran Formation (500±): White and pink quartzite with some shaly beds; grades downward into exactly similar Precambrian beds

Divided by some into Jonas Creek Formation above and Hector Formation below, but many local names. Massive quartzite of great thickness above, cliff-makers; shaly and slaty shale beds below (totals several thousand feet thick)

Note: Numbers in parentheses refer to thicknesses in feet
Modified from A.S.P.G. (1955, page 149)

Surface

AGE OF ROCKS

Mississippian

Devonian

Ordovician

Cambrian — Upper / Middle / Low.

Precambrian

GSC

Geological section: Banff park boundary to Jasper townsite.

22

patches of younger rocks lying in downfolds and preserved in mountain tops here and there. This system of valleys is also the route of the main Banff-Jasper highway. Further, the structures of the mountains seem to swing westward in the region of Jasper so that the Jasper-Yellowhead Pass road follows the same general structural trend and thus the same ancient rocks.

The lowest rocks in the column (see diagram) represent the oldest rocks in the park area, and these were laid down in the period of time referred to as the Precambrian. Rocks of Precambrian age in Jasper Park all seem to have been laid down in the latest part of the Precambrian, and in many places the record seems to extend from the Precambrian into the Cambrian period without any significant break or discontinuity. This is unusual, for all around the Canadian Shield there is a profound gap or interruption between the ancient Precambrian rocks and later ones.

The Precambrian rocks belong to two groups. The lower, and therefore the older one, is a sequence of several thousand metres of green and grey slaty shales with interbedded conglomerate and sandstone. This has been named the *Hector Formation*. The younger group overlies the Hector Formation and comprises several hundred metres of white and cream quartzitic sandstones with red and pink stains common in some layers, minor interbedded pebble layers, and shale lenses. These Precambrian rocks grade upward, almost imperceptibly, into early Cambrian quartzites, also several hundreds of metres thick. It is this vast accumulation of Precambrian and lower Cambrian slaty shale and quartzite that forms the mass of most of the mountains along the Banff-Jasper highway. Only a few are made of younger rocks. Mount Kerkeslin near Athabasca Falls, Mount Edith Cavell, Pyramid Mountain north of Jasper, the Signal-Tekarra-Antler mountain ridge, Mount Christie and adjacent peaks, and the long line of mountains of the Endless Chain Ridge—all of these are cut into these Precambrian and Cambrian rocks. Yellowhead Mountain and others of the continental divide area, including most of Mount Robson, are cut into the same rocks.

The quartzitic sandstones of lower Cambrian age are succeeded by 1,067 metres of limestone and dolomite of middle Cambrian and upper Cambrian age. These carbonate rocks belong to a number of formations that can be traced for many kilometres along the Rocky Mountain chain and are common in the Banff and Yoho areas in the sides of many of the famous peaks there. In the southern end of Jasper National Park they may be seen in the road-cuts on either side of the summit area, 13 kilometres north of the park entrance at Sunwapta Pass; in the great cliffs on the north end of Tangle Ridge; in the upper parts of Sunwapta Peak; and in many of the cliffs and peaks on the west side of the valley of the Sunwapta River, between Sunwapta Pass and a point opposite Tangle Ridge.

Rocks laid down in the next period of geological time, the *Ordovician* period, are referable to three principal formations. The bottom is the *Mons Formation*—nearly 305 metres of grey limestone grading upwards into shale. The next formation, the *Sarbach,* consists of shale in the lower part, and thick-bedded, cliff-forming limestone in the top, totalling more than 305 metres. A 120-metre unit of massive quartz sandstone, the *Mount Wilson Formation,* lies at the top of the Ordovician section.

Ordovician rocks are exposed in the southern end of Jasper Park from Sunwapta Pass entrance northward as far as the north end of Tangle Ridge. They outcrop along the road in the big cuts at the summit of the hill about 13 kilometres north of the south entrance. They form Wilcox Peak and the middle to upper slopes of Tangle Ridge. Rocks of the Silurian period are not widely known in Jasper Park.

Rocks laid down in the Devonian period belong to the *Fairholme Formation* and the succeeding *Alexo* and *Palliser* formations. The Fairholme consists of more than 400 metres of limestones. The Alexo, about 75 metres thick, is also a limestone formation. The Palliser limestone formation at the top is more than 500 metres thick and is famous throughout the Rocky Mountains as one of the great cliff-makers.

The only place to see the Devonian rocks near the road in the southern part of the park is again in the region from Tangle Ridge southward to the south entrance. The top of Tangle Ridge is in the Fairholme Formation, and abundant fossils may be found in the talus slopes on the south side. The grey cliffs in the lower part of

Nigel Peak, which looms to the north of the highway between the south boundary of the park and the Icefields Chalet, are in the Palliser Formation.

The youngest rocks in this axial part of Jasper National Park are of Mississippian age and are referable to two formations—the *Banff* and the *Rundle*. These are widely known in the oil fields under the plains, in the mountain peaks in the Banff region, and northward along the eastern side of the Rocky Mountains. The lower formation, the Banff, is more than 500 metres thick and comprises limestones and interbedded shales of brownish colour. It is exposed in the flank of Nigel Peak near the southern entrance of the park. The top of Nigel Peak is composed of a hundred metres of basal Rundle Formation—a great sequence of limestones that form cliffs in many places in Banff National Park.

Jasper and Eastward to Gate

The Jasper-Edmonton highway presents a view of the mountains that is altogether different from the one along the Banff-Jasper route. This is because the Jasper-Edmonton highway cuts across the ends of the mountain ridges along the Athabasca Valley, whereas the Banff road parallels the mountain structures. The rocks exposed in the mountains are also different.

In the Jasper area a great thickness of rocks laid down in the Precambrian and in the early part of the Cambrian period forms Pyramid Mountain, the Whistlers, Signal Mountain and Mount Tekarra. Eastward along the Jasper-Edmonton highway, however, the rocks represent several different periods of time—from the Precambrian upwards through the Cambrian, Ordovician, Silurian, Devonian, Mississippian, Triassic, Jurassic and Cretaceous. Because there are so many rock formations, we shall only describe them here in a general way.

The Cambrian is represented by 305 metres or so of limestone and dolomite with some shaly interbeds. Rocks of this age are rare in the area east of the Pyramid Mountain-Signal Mountain line. Rocks

Columbia Glacier is one of several tongues of ice that descend from the Columbia Icefield into the surrounding valleys. On the right is Mount Columbia. At 3,749 metres (12,294 feet) it is one of the highest in the Canadian Rockies.

of Ordovician and Silurian age are also known only rarely in this area, and these too are limestones with shaly layers.

Rocks of Devonian age form many of the mountains exposed in cross section along the valley of the Athabasca River east of Jasper. The lower 425 metres of the Devonian section consists of dolomite, limestone, shale, and siltstone, which are usually grey or black with some red and brown layers.

These rocks are capped by more than 245 metres of massive grey limestone of the *Palliser Formation,* widely known all over the Rocky Mountains as a cliff-former. Where the Devonian rocks are strongly folded, this grey limestone makes impressive sweeping lines on the fronts of the mountains, such as on Roche à Bosche, Roche Ronde, and Esplanade Mountain. Grey cliffs of Palliser limestone form the peak of Roche Miette, the long scarp of the Palisade, the uppermost slopes of Roche de Smet, and steeply dipping slopes on the west side of Ashlar Ridge and on the Colin Range.

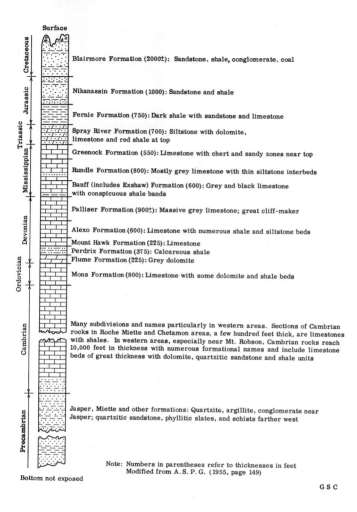

Surface

Blairmore Formation (2000±): Sandstone, shale, conglomerate, coal

Nikanassin Formation (1000): Sandstone and shale

Fernie Formation (750): Dark shale with sandstone and limestone

Spray River Formation (700): Siltstone with dolomite, limestone and red shale at top

Greenock Formation (550): Limestone with chert and sandy zones near top

Rundle Formation (800): Mostly grey limestone with thin siltstone interbeds

Banff (includes Exshaw) Formation (600): Grey and black limestone with conspicuous shale bands

Palliser Formation (900±): Massive grey limestone; great cliff-maker

Alexo Formation (600): Limestone with numerous shale and siltstone beds

Mount Hawk Formation (225): Limestone
Perdrix Formation (375): Calcareous shale
Flume Formation (225): Grey dolomite

Mons Formation (800): Limestone with some dolomite and shale beds

Many subdivisions and names particularly in western areas. Sections of Cambrian rocks in Roche Miette and Chetamon areas, a few hundred feet thick, are limestones with shales. In western areas, especially near Mt. Robson, Cambrian rocks reach 10,000 feet in thickness with numerous formational names and include limestone beds of great thickness with dolomite, quartzitic sandstone and shale units

Jasper, Miette and other formations: Quartzite, argillite, conglomerate near Jasper; quartzitic sandstone, phyllitic slates, and schists farther west

Note: Numbers in parentheses refer to thicknesses in feet
Modified from A. S. P. G. (1955, page 149)

Bottom not exposed

(Vertical axis labels, top to bottom: Cretaceous, Jurassic, Triassic, Mississippian, Devonian, Ordovician, Cambrian, Precambrian)

GSC

Geological section: Jasper and eastward to gate.

The Mississippian period of geological time is widely represented in the complex mountain structures in the eastern section of Jasper National Park. The *Banff Formation,* and the *Rundle Formation* above it, are limestone-and-shale units which can be traced all along the Rocky Mountain System. In the neighbourhood of Banff they make up the bulk of Mount Rundle and Cascade Mountain. Here in Jasper, 258 kilometres to the northwest, they are readily recognizable in the peak of Cinquefoil Mountain, in the peaks about Esplanade and Chetamon mountains, and in the front of the Colin Range to the north of Jasper. The latest rocks of the Mississippian period belong to the *Greenock Formation* and may be seen lying above the Banff and Rundle formations although they are not as conspicuous in most places.

Triassic, Jurassic and Cretaceous rocks consist largely of shales and siltstones with interbedded limestone and dolomite units, occasional sandstones, and, in the Cretaceous, seams of coal. Patches of the Triassic are found enfolded with the underlying Carboniferous in some of the upper mountains, but the younger rocks almost all occur in the valleys only. This may seem a reversal of the law of superposition which says that in any sequence of sedimentary rocks the youngest should be on top. But it becomes understandable when we realize that the mountains here consist of a series of *fault blocks* thrust up over one another, in a manner described and illustrated in the section "Regional Differences in the Mountains."

The Sculpturing of the Mountains

As soon as the rocks were laid bare by the retreat of the seas in which they were laid down, they were subjected to the ever-present erosive action of rain, running water, falling snow, moving ice, frost, and chemical decay. Of all these agents of erosion, running water has been by far the most important in the carving of the mountains as we know them. For millions of years streams have carried away the debris of all the other agents of decay and erosion, and have themselves carved their valleys deep into the landscape.

The Columbia Glacier spills over a great rock cliff from the Columbia Icefield. The foreground is rock rubble on a lateral moraine, pushed up when the glacier filled much more of the valley than it does now.

The story of water erosion may begin on the highest peak. The freezing of a thin film of water under a boulder may wedge it out and tumble it over the edge of a cliff. Heavy rains may loosen rocks and boulders or may lubricate others so that they too join the downward rush. Thus, bits and pieces of rocks are torn from the solid mountains and begin their long journey to the sea.

Their first resting place may be in one of the long fan-shaped accumulations of angular blocks and pieces of rock which we can see on the sides of every steep mountain. These are called *talus* or *scree* slopes, and their steepness is generally the maximum angle at which the loose rubble is stable. Climbing on them may be very difficult, particularly on the lower parts which consist of very large angular boulders and chunks of rock lying in all attitudes where they have rolled or fallen. This means that not only will the surface of the talus or scree slope be very rough and irregular, but slight disturbances— even the passing weight of a man—may cause more sliding and adjustment of the blocks and particles in it.

Rivers may wash the bottoms of the talus slopes and carry off some of the boulders and rubble, so that angular pieces and fragments from the talus now become part of the mass of boulders, gravel, and sand in the bottoms of stream valleys. Constant rubbing of boulders and pebbles against one another gradually wears them down, and the fragments become very finely divided rock flour that looks like mud or silt in the water of the stream. Thus, over the ages, the mass of rocks in the mountains is gradually worn away by the

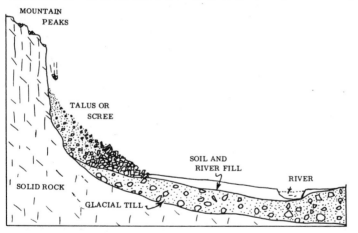

A common sequence of erosion in Rocky Mountain country begins when boulders and smaller particles of rock are wedged off the bare rocky peaks and fall to the talus or scree slopes below. Physical and chemical breakdown of the rocks in the talus produces fine-grained materials which move in the wash of rain and in streams, towards the river. A layer of glacial till made of a mixture of boulders, sand and clay commonly blankets the solid rock underneath the soil and river-fill in such valleys. In many places the glacial till is actively eroded by the river and thus contributes directly to the load of sediments on its way to the distant sea.

forces of erosion and carried ultimately to the sea, where it rests on the bottom as mud, silt, or sand.

After a very long period, during which great valleys were carved and the main outlines of the mountains as we know them were shaped by the action of running water, there came a period when the whole of northern North America was covered by a great icecap, rather like those on Antarctica and Greenland today. This period of glaciation began about a million years ago and lasted until quite recent times, perhaps ten thousand years ago.

Glacier erosion is of two kinds. When an area is covered by an icecap, more or less evenly, the movement of ice outward from the centre of accumulation of snow tends to round off the bumps and smooth out the hollows. High in the mountains, however, the action of the glaciers is generally much more localized and accentuated. Around the margins of snowfields or icefields, glaciers push down the valleys, steepening them and deepening them as they go. In the areas of accumulation, great bowl-shaped depressions—called *cirques*—are sometimes carved deep into the mountainsides. These commonly have almost vertical back walls and rounded bottoms. The cutting action caused by the movement of ice and snow toward the centres of cirques and the outlets of snowfields tends to steepen the scenery in the mountains and make it much more sharp and angular. If, for example, cirques are being cut into two opposite sides of a mountain, the two vertical back walls may happen to intersect one another, leaving a razor-sharp rock ridge. It sometimes happens that a rounded mountain peak of considerable elevation is cut into by cirques from several sides. This process may leave semi-pyramidal towers of rock, like the world-famous Matterhorn, or Mount Assiniboine in the Canadian Rockies.

Long tongues of ice extending from snowfields down the valleys as valley glaciers commonly steepen the valley walls, pushing great piles of rock rubble and debris ahead of them. The position of maximum penetration of such alpine glaciers is commonly marked by great heaps of the debris they have left behind. Long *finger lakes* are sometimes found in such dammed-up valleys, but in others the river was able to cut through the dam and drain the upper valley.

Right: The Snake Indian Falls.

Below: The head of the Athabasca River is in this braided stream system. The water on the left, as you look at the picture, comes from the melting of the Columbia Glacier and is clear because its silt has settled out in a small lake at the foot of the glacier. That on the right comes directly from melting ice and is grey with glacial silt, so that it shows very light in this aerial view.

Farther back, where the valley walls were much steepened, a characteristic U-shape is impressed on the valley and the bottom is covered with a blanket of glacial debris. Small streams, occupying shallow valleys on the shoulders of the main valleys, may now tumble over the edge in very high waterfalls. The high valleys that the streams run in are called *hanging valleys.*

Thus we can see how glaciers tend to sharpen the profiles of mountains and make the scenery more angular. Bowl-shaped depressions with vertical walls (*cirques*), sharp ridges with nearly vertical sides, sharp angular mountain peaks, U-shaped and hanging valleys—all of these are characteristic of areas of upland glaciation. Nowadays, in Canada's western mountains, we can see a few remnants of the ice that covered the whole area in the not very distant geological past as the glaciers and snowfields still left on the heights and in protected places.

In the few thousands of years since the glaciers modified the shape of Canada's western mountains, rivers have resumed the carving and cutting of the great mass of uplifted rock. Now, however, their valleys are choked with glacial debris brought from higher places by the moving ice. In some places the cirques or bowl-shaped depressions carved by the glaciers are occupied by small lakes called *tarns,* and in other places the long valleys have filled with water and are now long finger lakes.

The glacial litter—the vast quantity of sand, gravel, and ground-up rock—is in some places distributed and redistributed by flowing rivers over flat valley floors to make *braided* streams, as in the uppermost Athabasca and Sunwapta rivers. Steep rock walls and cliffs abound. In summer, when meltwaters from the glaciers and the snowfields make the rivers high, you can imagine what an enormous load of rock debris is being carried to the sea each year from the wasting mountains.

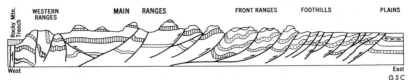

West   East
                                                                             G S C

This cross section through the Rocky Mountains, from the Plains to their western boundary, is greatly simplified to show the main features of their structural framework. In the east (the right in the diagram) flat-lying sedimentary rocks lie under the Plains layer upon layer, thousands of metres thick. In the Foothills the rocks are broken into steeply dipping slices, tilted so that each layer dips to the west, and uplifted so that rocks are brought from the depths up to or close to the surface.

The Front Ranges are made of slices of severely folded and faulted rocks which are uplifted and eroded so that layers that once were deep beneath the Plains are now at the surface, and in the valleys older rocks may be seen lying on top of younger rocks along each of the fault planes.

The simpler Main Ranges of the Rocky Mountains lie to the west of the complicated structures of the Front Ranges. They are cut into masses of sedimentary rocks which have not been severely folded but have been uplifted high into the air. Erosion has stripped off younger rocks, and today we can see the flat-lying older rocks high in the peaks.

The Western Ranges are cut into fractured and folded younger rocks. The western boundary of the Rocky Mountains is the Rocky Mountain Trench, indicated by the dotted pattern. It is filled with thick deposits of sands and gravels and is occupied by major rivers like the Kootenay, the Columbia and the Fraser.

34

Regional Differences in the Mountains

The western mountains of Canada show a distinct zoning from east to west at many different places along their length. Undisturbed flat-lying rocks underlie the western plains from Manitoba to near the western boundary of Alberta. To the west this area is succeeded by the *Foothills,* a region of folded and faulted rocks which have not been greatly uplifted. Still farther west, the *Front Ranges* of the Rocky Mountains succeed the Foothills along a very sharply marked boundary line. The Front Ranges are made of a series of fault slices of folded and broken rocks thrust together so that they overlap like the shingles on a roof.

The region of the Front Ranges is separated fairly clearly from another zone of mountains to the west—the *Main Ranges* of the Rocky Mountains. Here, the rocks at the surface are relatively un-disturbed although very much uplifted and deeply eroded. This we can tell because they include some of the oldest rocks exposed in the Rocky Mountain System. Farther west again are the *Western Ranges* of the Rocky Mountain System, built along a belt of severe distur-bance in which the rocks are broken, faulted, and severely folded.

In Jasper National Park we find only the Front Ranges and the Main Ranges of the Rocky Mountains; the Foothills lie to the east of the park boundary and the Western Ranges disappear along the edge of the Rocky Mountain Trench before getting this far north.

The Front Ranges consist of a series of northwest-trending fault blocks of folded and broken rocks of Devonian to Triassic age. Each slice or block is composed of folded and faulted rocks that have rid-den up over older rocks along westward-dipping fault surfaces. Ero-sion has cut deeply into the complicated pattern of rocks thus pro-duced to make the present array of mountains and valleys. Resistant layers make peaks, weak layers make valleys and lowlands. In many places the valleys are underlain by younger rocks with upthrust older rocks forming the mountains on each side.

This arrangement of thrust blocks is apparent all along the road from the park gate below Roche à Perdrix to the Palisade not far east of Jasper. Each of the major groups of peaks visible from the road along the valley bottom is, in fact, the end of one of these fault slices.

In this region, four more or less discrete units may be recognized. Near the entrance, Fiddle Range on the southeast side of the river is matched by Bedson Ridge on the northwest side. Bosche Range on the northwest side of the Athabasca River and Miette Range and others to the southeast form another structural unit. These are separated from the next group, the Jacques - de Smet Range, by the broad valley of Snake Indian River and its continuation on the other side of the Athabasca River, occupied by the Rocky River. The group nearest to Jasper includes Colin Range and the Esplanade-Chetamon mountain ridges.

Off to the southeast the distinction between the units of the Front Ranges becomes less clear, although the mountains still look like great windrows on the surface of the earth. The structure within the masses is also the same, and sweeping lines of folded and faulted rocks stand out clearly in the walls of any of the valleys that cross the trend of the mountains.

A great fault, called by some the *Castle Mountain Thrust,* runs the length of Jasper National Park and separates the Front Ranges from the Main Ranges, which are characterized by a different kind of mountain structure. This great break or series of breaks enters the park from the northwest, crosses the upper Snake Indian River near the double bend below Mount Simla, and follows southeasterly toward the valley of the Snaring River. It follows along the southwestward side of that valley a short distance from the river itself and separates the ridge of the Palisade from the main bulk of Pyramid Mountain to the southwest. Southeastward across the Athabasca River the fault follows the northeastern slope of Maligne Range, passes south and west of Maligne Lake and along the upper valley of Poboktan Creek towards the boundary of the park. Some geologists believe that this same fault zone underlies Mount Eisenhower in Banff National Park and the block of mountains that includes Mount Assiniboine, still farther south.

The mountains to the southwest of this enormous fracture in the crust of the earth—the Main Ranges—are quite different from those in the Front Ranges. They include all the famous peaks along the Continental Divide from Mount Assiniboine, south of Banff, to Mount Robson, northwest of Jasper and, when one comes to think of it, the peaks do have a similarity of appearance because they are all cut into uplifted and gently tilted sedimentary rocks.

A gentle downwarp or *syncline* parallels the western side of the Castle Mountain Thrust from Mount Eisenhower (which used to be called Castle Mountain, and from which the fault is named) north-westward to Mount Kerkeslin, opposite Athabasca Falls on the main Banff-Jasper highway. All along this structure the rocks dip gently southwestward into it from the northeast side and gently northeast-ward into it from the southwest side. In the very centre the rocks are flat-lying. Mount Kerkeslin is a remnant of the very centre or *axis* of this downfold and its structure can be clearly seen from the Athabasca Falls area and from several points along the highway to the northwest. Another part of the syncline or downfold structure is even more clearly visible from the main highway about halfway be-tween the bridge over Poboktan Creek and the Sunwapta Falls road junction. In this section the mountains on each side are obviously made of rocks that dip inwards toward the valley bottom.

The younger rocks present in the area of Tangle Ridge, Wilcox Peak and Nigel Peak near the southern end of Jasper Park occur where they do because the syncline or downfold sags in this area. This means that the older rocks on the sides plunge more deeply into the earth and the surface is made of younger rocks in the centre of the trough.

The structures in the rocks change as you move away from this long syncline, and may be said to be a series of gentle upfolds and downfolds or *anticlines* and *synclines,* to use the technical terms. Thus, in each of the peaks the rock layers may be seen to be dipping gently one way or another, depending on just where they are in rela-tion to the individual folds of which they are a part. So it is that they all have the same general appearance but depend on the accidents of erosion and the particular layers they are cut into for their charac-teristic shapes and colouring.

Shapes of Mountains

Travellers in the mountains have long noted the distinctive shapes of individual mountains. These are due to a combination of three things: the kinds of rocks that go to make up the mountain, the structure of the rocks within the mountain, and the particular tools or agents of erosion which have carved the mountain (in the case of the mountains in Canada's western parks, the rivers and glaciers). An assortment of rock types which vary from flat-lying to vertical and from parallel-layered to crumpled and folded, has contributed to the many different shapes of the mountains we see in Jasper Park. The hundreds of peaks and mountain masses, however, belong to only about eight kinds—the ones given in the examples here.

Castellate, Castle, or Layer-cake Mountains

Mountains that are cut into more or less flat-lying sedimentary rocks commonly have profiles in which vertical steps alternate with flat or sloping terraces. Some such mountains look very much like ancient castles and are thus said to be *castellate* or *castle* mountains. Mountains of this kind are best developed in regions underlain by great thicknesses of rocks in which beds of massive limestone and sandstone or quartzite alternate with less resistant shale or slate beds. The softer beds are eroded more rapidly, so that the harder beds are undermined and tend to break off at right angles, forming steep slopes and cliffs. Steep-sided needles and pinnacles are sometimes left on the tops of such mountains as the uppermost massive layers are cut away. The Ramparts, Yellowhead Mountain, and several of the mountains near Mount Christie are examples. Mount Eisenhower in Banff National Park so impressed early travellers that they called it Castle Mountain.

Mountains Cut in Dipping Layered Rocks

Some mountain peaks are cut into masses of layered sedimentary rocks which *dip* or slope from nearly horizontal to 50 or 60 degrees.

Castellate

Anticlinal

Dogtooth

Dipping layered

Synclinal

Matterhorn

Sawtooth

Complex structure

39

Some of these, like Endless Chain Ridge or Sunwapta Peak, have one smooth slope which follows the dip of a particular rock layer from its peak almost to its base, and, on the other side, a less regular slope which breaks across the upturned edges of the layered rock units. Other mountains, like Mount Edith Cavell, are cut into dipping sedimentary rocks in such a way that neither side follows the dipping rock layers, and thus both sides are irregular.

Dogtooth Mountains

Sharp jagged mountains sometimes result from the erosion of masses of vertical or nearly vertical rock. The peaks may be centred on a particularly resistant bed, in which case a tall spine or rock wall may result. Cinquefoil Mountain and some small peaks in the Front Ranges are of this kind.

Sawtooth Mountains

If the rocks in a long ridge are vertical, erosion may produce rows of angular mountains that look like the teeth in a saw. This type can be seen in the Sawback Range near Mount Eisenhower in Banff National Park, the Colin Range east of Jasper, and the mountains northeast of Medicine Lake.

Irregular Mountains

Many mountains are cut into more or less homogeneous masses of rock and as a result have no particularly characteristic shapes. These we may call *irregular mountains,* although individual peaks may be round, conical, pyramidal, or quite shapeless, depending on how they were cut.

Synclinal Mountains

Mountains are very commonly cut by erosion into masses of rocks that have been folded into great arches and troughs. Erosion over long periods may cut away all the surrounding rocks to leave a mountain with a trough or bowl structure within it. This probably comes about because the folded rocks in the centre of the trough, which is called a *syncline,* are more resistant to erosion than those in the surrounding parts, which tend to split and break during folding. Mount Kerkeslin in Jasper National Park is an excellent example of a synclinal mountain.

Anticlinal Mountains

In some regions of folded rocks, mountains are underlain by great up-bowed or arched masses of rock. Such upfolds are *anticlines* and the mountains are called *anticlinal mountains.* Stretching of the rocks on the outside or upper layers results in numerous fractures which in turn make the rocks very susceptible to erosion, so that true anticlinal mountains are rare.

Mountains of Complex Structure

Anticlines and synclines, that is upfolds and downfolds, may be seen in the flanks of some mountains that have been developed on tightly folded rocks. These we may call *complex mountains* because of the complex structure of the rocks within them. Magnificent examples can be seen all along the eastern edge of Jasper National Park.

Matterhorn Mountains

When glaciers cut deeply into rocks that are more or less homogeneous they carve bowl-shaped depressions called *cirques.* When several cirques cut into a mountain mass but are stopped by a warming of the climate and consequent melting, they sometimes leave sharp, semi-pyramidal towers of rock to which the general term *matterhorn* is given. Mount Assiniboine is an outstanding example in the Canadian Rockies.

Places of Particular Geological Interest

Underground Drainage in the Maligne River Valley

Limestone is easily dissolved in rain water. In limestone areas that have considerable relief it is common for surface water to disappear into the ground along cracks and fissures, to form underground streams. These reappear as springs and seeps somewhere lower down. Once underground, the water works its way downward into the rocks and dissolves the limestone, and thus enlarges the openings so that more and more of the surface water joins the underground system.

That part of Jasper National Park northeast of Maligne Range and the mountains along the southwest shore of Maligne Lake is underlain by limestone beds and stands well above the level of the Athabasca River valley to the northwest. One would expect some evidences of underground-water activity in this region.

A trip along the main road to Medicine Lake or a look at a map of the region will show some unusual things. For example, when you get close to the end of Medicine Lake from Jasper, the water in the Maligne River seems to disappear; and during much of the year the upper end of the Maligne River, just below Medicine Lake, consists of a dry streambed between scattered pools. At the other end of Medicine Lake you will see a rushing river entering the lake. Where does the water go? Some of it is used to fill up the basin of Medicine Lake, which becomes almost empty during the late fall and winter. Some of it must go underground.

Evidence of a large underground drainage system is found about 16 kilometres to the northwest in the lower end of Maligne Canyon. Viewers of the canyon (see page 46) may be struck by how much more water seems to come out of its lower end than goes into the upper end. The reason is that a very large part of what comes out of the lower end of the canyon has come into the river from huge springs near the end of the canyon itself. Now where does it go into the underground drainage system? We go back to Medicine Lake for part of

The Maligne River is little more than a brook at this spot just below the road crossing and tea room. Note how the limestone bedrock dips gently westward.

the answer and into some of the valleys east of the Medicine Lake-Maligne Lake road for more evidence.

Medicine Lake has an unusual seasonal variation. In July and August, when most of the visitors come, it is an ordinary-looking lake with beautiful scenery all around. The water level, however, begins to drop in September and October as the amount of water from melting snow in the mountains decreases. By November the lake is almost completely gone, and wide areas of sandy and silty flats with pools and distributaries of the river coming in from the south corner are all that remain. The local warden says that underground falls can clearly be heard and that the water can be seen going underground in several places. The inlets appear to be principally along the northeast side, with several near the cove leading to the Beaver Lake

valley at the southeast corner of the lake. Travelling over the shrivelled remains of the lake is dangerous in winter because of the distributaries and flats and the occasional deep holes.

In early summer, the melting snows on the mountains all around begin to pour water into the Medicine Lake basin once again and raise its level several metres. In seasons of heavy runoff, the lake fills up enough to spill over into the outlet brook and enter the lower Maligne river system directly. Then the autumn shrinkage sets in again and the cycle is repeated.

And what of the future of Medicine Lake? "Precarious and very temporary" would describe it. All lakes are temporary interruptions of the normal drainage of an area and last only as long as it takes the outlets to cut down low enough to drain them. But the future of Medicine Lake depends more on how fast the underground drainage channels are enlarged by solution and wear, for as soon as they are large enough to take all the water that comes into the lake basin, even in the highest floods, then Medicine Lake will no longer fill up in summer.

This is not the only place in the region where drainage goes underground. In the Queen Elizabeth Ranges the valley that lies parallel to the Maligne River between the lakes has several low areas with brooks coming in and nothing going out on the surface. Two small lakes lie in the deepest parts of the valley, and they too have drainage coming in from all sides but no apparent outlets. There is only one answer to where the water goes: into the underground drainage system.

The trend of the rock formations in the direction of Medicine Lake and the elevation of even the lowest parts of the valley, some 300 metres above Medicine Lake level, make it seem likely that the water from this valley finds its way underground, into the subterranean Maligne system, under Medicine Lake and eventually into the lower Maligne River.

Solution of limestone by this large volume of underground water has almost certainly produced large caves and underground passages. Someday an entrance to them may be found so that a whole new underground wonderland can be explored.

Maligne Canyon

The drainage from a valley system about 80 kilometres long and 10 to 16 kilometres wide empties into the Athabasca River via the Maligne River a little more than 5 kilometres below the village of Jasper, at an elevation of about 1,006 metres (3,300 feet) above sea level. Its principal reservoir is Maligne Lake, about 40 kilometres above its mouth and 1,674 metres (5,490 feet) above sea level. The river thus has an average gradient of about 15 metres per kilometre, which is very steep. Medicine Lake lies in the course of the river about 16 kilometres above its mouth at an elevation of 1,448 metres (4,750 feet) above sea level.

The upper end of the Maligne River is a normal fast-flowing stream that derives its water from melting snows on the mountains all around. When the water of the Maligne River enters Medicine Lake, however, its behaviour is no longer ordinary, for some of it is held there in storage while the bulk of it disappears into the underground drainage system. This has already been described in some detail.

In times of very high water, usually midsummer, Medicine Lake spills directly into the river valley that leads toward the Athabasca River. At other times the drainage is by a variety of underground routes, some leading to the surface and adding their volume to the lower Maligne River. For some distance below Medicine Lake the river gathers volume from underground sources and from the surface drainage of the neighbouring hills. Just below the roadbridge at the Maligne Canyon tea room the river is seen to be fast flowing and eroding the limestone bedrock by wearing against its left bank and tearing out boulders and pieces as it follows the dip of the rock formations. In this section, too, may be seen numerous round *potholes* and parts of potholes. These are cut in the bedrock by the stream as it moves boulders round and round in its swift currents, and they may be cylindrical, jug-shaped or almost any shape, with smooth, rounded walls.

A hundred metres below this, the stream has cut a steep-walled canyon a few metres deep as it begins its plunge to the level of the

Right: The swirling waters of the Maligne River have produced the potholes and curved surfaces seen here.

Below: Maligne Canyon is cut into the limestones of the Palliser Formation. In this view, the curved walls show where potholes and solution surfaces were formed, while the more angular and rugged parts show later weathering and places where rocks have fallen out. A footbridge with people viewing the scene is just visible at the top of the picture.

Athabasca River valley below. The first footbridge is built at a point from which all the water in the river literally squirts out of a round orifice, spreads in mid-air and drops some 23 metres to the bottom of the deeper canyon.

Above the bridge an old pothole can be seen in section view with some of the gravel and boulders the stream used long ago to cut it. The swirling action of the water can be seen in the canyon bottom, and one can easily imagine how boulders caught in the currents are swept round and round, gouging larger and deeper potholes as they grind away at the sides and bottoms. Protuberances would be worn away because they would be more fiercely abraded and more quickly dissolved in their more exposed positions. All down through the canyon the curved surfaces formed in this way may be seen on the rock walls. The walls of the canyon also show how joints or breaks in the limestones have controlled erosion. In some places the rock has broken away from the walls along joint planes.

Just below the first (uppermost) bridge the volume of the stream is split in two. The left branch will probably take over the whole volume as it cuts lower and lower, leaving the right side high and dry. Farther downstream the canyon is very narrow in places and boulders are jammed between the walls. These have either fallen from above or been undermined and dropped to their present positions.

Downstream from the first bridge, the bottom of the canyon drops lower and lower in a series of falls and rapids with smoother stretches between. The water drops about 120 metres in the course of one and a half kilometres, but the canyon itself is nowhere more than 60 metres deep because the regional slope of the land is also fairly steep, as one can tell from walking along the edge of the canyon on the footpaths.

After a walk along the canyon and a visit to the lower end, it is not difficult to imagine how the canyon was cut. In recent geological times, the Maligne River was pushed out of its course by glaciation so that it flowed over the edge of the escarpment on the side of the glaciated and altered Athabasca River valley. The easily eroded limestone was soon deeply cut into by solution and abrasion in the fast-flowing waters.

47

A view of the lower and upper ends of the gorge on the same day cannot fail to impress the visitor because of the very great difference in volume of water; the amount of rushing water in the river opposite the fish hatchery is several times that at the tea room bridge just above the head of the canyon. Much water must flow into the Maligne River from underground sources in the lower end of the canyon. It is intriguing to think that some of it may have come more than 40 kilometres in a series of subterranean channels and caves.

The grey limestone into which the canyon is cut belongs to the Palliser Formation, laid down in the Devonian period of geological time. This is an important rock unit, for it forms great cliffs in the mountains from south of Banff northward to beyond Jasper. A great wall of Palliser limestone is readily seen in the east face of the Palisade just across the Athabasca River Valley from Maligne Canyon.

The Palliser Formation dips at 5 to 10 degrees in a westward direction in the area of the upper canyon, so that one would look for overlying younger rocks to the west and older rocks underneath it to the east. Shaly limestone and dark shales of the younger Banff Formation, laid down in the Mississippian period, may be seen at several places below the canyon and westward of it. The dip is a little steeper below the canyon where the Maligne River follows more or less along the Palliser-Banff boundary.

Miette Hot Springs

Hot springs are known in many different parts of the world and have intrigued people ever since they were first discovered thousands of years ago. Curative powers have often been attributed to them, sometimes with some basis in the minerals and gases dissolved in them and sometimes not. Miette Hot Springs, at the end of the branch road near the east gate on the Jasper-Edmonton highway, is one of many groups of hot springs found along the Rocky Mountains from Mexico to Alaska.

The water issuing from these springs starts originally as rain or snow on the surface of the ground. It is thought that it percolates into the rocks, along fissures and cracks and through pore spaces, deep enough to come into contact with hot rock masses where it is heated and charged with many substances in solution. In some places it may even be turned to steam and rise toward the surface again, near which it condenses in the cooler rocks and issues as springs from cracks and openings of its own solution. In others, the water probably stays in the liquid phase throughout its underground history and emerges somewhere lower down than the intake area, in the same way that ordinary springs do.

Miette Hot Springs occurs as a series of springs and minor *leaks* in the narrow and steep-walled valley of Sulphur Creek, a short distance above the swimming pool facilities. The waters are piped to the pool by simple gravity flow. The three principal springs and several smaller ones supply water that comes out at various temperatures, but the hottest one, at about 52°C (126°F), is the hottest of all springs in the Canadian Rockies. The daily combined flow is about 568,245 litres (125,000 gallons).

If you travel up the brook valley above the pool area to the springs themselves, you may note that yellow and grey deposits are formed around the orifices. Calcium and magnesium sulphate are the most abundant of the dissolved substances in the hot-spring waters, with minor quantities of calcium bicarbonate and hydrogen sulphide. In addition to these, small amounts of iron, manganese, boron, silica, and potassium, and the gases nitrogen, carbon dioxide, argon, and helium are also present. Minute traces of radium, and radon which comes from the radioactive disintegration of radium, occur in these as in all the hot springs of western Canada.

Nobody knows exactly where the water comes from, but the position of the springs area on the faulted central or axial part of an anticline suggests some sort of structural control of the underground migration of the water. You can see large patches of spongy calcareous rock, and fragments of limestone cemented by the same spongy calcareous rock, along the valley walls in the vicinity of the springs. Spongy rock of this kind is deposited by hot springs, so these masses tell us that springs have been active in other parts of the valley at other times.

Columbia Icefield

The Columbia Icefield is an area of some 389 square kilometres (150 square miles) of glacial ice and snow astride the Continental Divide at the southern end of Jasper National Park and adjacent parts of Banff National Park and Hamber Provincial Park of British Columbia. If you could stand on its summit, you would get an idea of what the whole area of northern North America must have looked like when it was covered with an icecap in geologically recent times, for the wintry scene extends in all directions for many kilometres and is only broken here and there by the higher peaks sticking out as *nunataks* or rock islands.

Tongues of ice from the Columbia Icefield move down three principal valleys, as the Athabasca Glacier to the northeast, the Saskatchewan Glacier to the east, and the Columbia Glacier to the northwest. Numerous other smaller outlets from the central reservoir spill over into the surrounding valleys. Dome Glacier, just north of Athabasca Glacier in Jasper National Park, is formed of ice that tumbles over the edge of the cliffs at the back of its valley and then is reconstituted as a solid mass. The rim of the Columbia Icefield can be seen from several points along the highway north of the Athabasca Glacier, and spectacular icefalls and reconstituted glaciers below them may be seen in places such as below Mount Kitchener and Stutfield Peak.

The Columbia Icefield covers the three-way divide point described in an earlier section on ''Divides'' and thus contributes to three great river systems. The Athabasca River flows more than 1,200 kilometres to the northeast to join the Mackenzie river system and continue to the Arctic Ocean. The North Saskatchewan River, whose waters flow more than 1,900 kilometres to empty into Hudson Bay, begins in the meltwaters of Saskatchewan Glacier. Meltwaters from the western slope of the Columbia Icefield feed tributaries high up in the Columbia river system, which flows 1,930 kilometres to the Pacific Ocean.

The Columbia Icefield supplies the substance of Athabasca Glacier, seen here from two different viewpoints. Compare these pictures with what you see now, for there are continual changes in the details of the valley as well as the ice.

Above: In the summer of 1960, this gush of milky, silt-laden water issued from a cave under the ice on the north side of the foot of Athabasca Glacier.
Below: This is not what one would normally associate with the surface of a glacier, yet it is typical of part of the western edge of Athabasca Glacier.

Athabasca Glacier

The Athabasca Glacier, at the south end of Jasper National Park, is one of the few places in the world where you can step out of a car within a few metres of an active glacier. During the tourist season there are trips by snowmobile over the ice along the main stream of the glacier for several kilometres, where you can see many glacial features formerly accessible only to mountain climbers and travellers in remote places. The view from the centre of the Athabasca Glacier is utterly spectacular, with its dark cliffs, dazzling white ice in the tributary glaciers on its sides, and the great three-step icefall at the back.

The best viewpoint for an overall appreciation of the Athabasca Glacier is on the flank of Wilcox Peak, up the hill and north of the Icefields Chalet. From here the white expanse of the main body of the Columbia Icefield is visible at the back of the glacier. The ice flows over three great icefalls that look like three terraces at the head of the Athabasca Glacier. During much of the year, fresh snow obscures the fractured and crevassed surfaces of the icefalls, but a clear view of the broken ice may be had in the late summer.

The main tongue of ice fills a great trough-shaped valley to a depth of about 300 metres over some of its length, with a gradual thinning toward the end or the foot of the glacier. The glacier is wider than it looks in the lower reaches, for it extends underneath the dark rubble-covered areas on each side. The waste-covered area is especially wide on the north side (the right side as you face the glacier).

The view from back of the chalet or from the chalet itself is also impressive because of the amount of rock waste in irregular piles and in ridges. The largest of these is along the south or left side as you face the glacier, with several smaller ones cutting across the foreground with narrow gaps marking places where the roads go through them. These are all deposits of glacial debris made when the Athabasca Glacier was larger than it is now. Some believe this to have been at the most recent ice maximum, which took place about 1890. Since then the melting has been greater than the addition of ice from the back so that the glacier has gradually shrunk from these marginal and terminal ridges to its present position.

The view from the end of the road at the ice-front is impressive for other reasons. Patches of fresh white snow from the past winter contrast with the darker glacial ice. The sound of running water is everywhere as the glacier melts in the summer's heat. Open cracks or *crevasses* mark the forward edge of the glacier in several directions. Channels cut into the surface by the meltwater show solid, pale blue or blue-green ice beneath the granular and often dirty surface.

Visitors to this part of the glacier are surprised when they step out of their cars on fine warm days with no special winds blowing elsewhere, to be greeted by a steady blast of cool air. The air over the glacier is cooled by its contact with the ice. Cool air, being heavier than warm air, tends to sink into it. Thus, the air on the surface of the glacier, which is heavier than the warmer air in the valley at the foot of the glacier, tends to slide down the surface of the ice and into the bottom of the valley. This makes the wind, and because of its origin it has only a very local effect.

A trip over the surface of the glacier by snowmobile or on foot is a rewarding experience, for it allows close inspection of many of the features of glaciers. Crevasses reveal the solid, pale blue-green ice in depth, and the colour is sometimes very beautiful as it is intensified by repeated reflections back and forth between the sides. The melt-water streams cut through the surface debris and the granular ice on top to reveal the same glacial ice. Dark stones and pebbles may be seen set several centimetres into the surface because they absorb the sun's heat and melt their way into the ice. In other spots, larger boulders are perched on pillars of ice because they have protected the ice immediately under them from melting in the sun's warmth or in the warm summer rains.

On the southern flank of the Athabasca Glacier two masses of ice are perched on the walls of the valley. These come from the ac-cumulation of snow at their heads and from the refreezing together of blocks of ice that tumble over the edge from the icefield above. Conspicuous banding, representing seasons, is visible in some of the fronts of these where spalling has produced cross sections. At places

When Athabasca Glacier filled the entire valley, vast quantities of rock rubble came off the side to form the ridge seen right of centre. As the ice retreated with the warming of the climate, this ridge was left behind.

where the slowly moving ice is not able to accommodate itself to the rough rock terrain underneath, the ice splits along crevasses which may intersect one another to produce groups of great ice splinters or *seracs*. These may be seen in the three terracelike icefalls at the back of the Athabasca Glacier as well as in the two valleyside glaciers.

It is interesting to note that the two valleyside glacial masses on the south side of the Athabasca Glacier continued all the way down to the main glacier a very few years ago. With increased wastage due to a warming climate, they are now left hanging on the sides with piles of mixed rock rubble and ice in cones below them.

In summer the surface of the glacier is covered with meltwater

Fragments of rock that fall on the surfaces of glaciers vary in shape and size. Some broad ones act as parasols, protecting the ice below from the sun's heat and from summer rains, so that they are left on pedestals like this one.

streams which flow off the sides and over the front. Some of these flow along straight lines that are probably resealed cracks. Others flow irregularly along the top of the glacier and then fall noisily into crevasses to join the water flowing along underneath the ice. The outlet for the subglacial water changes as the glacier changes through the years. In 1960, a very large stream of subglacial water poured out of an ice cave on the north side of the meltwater lake at the foot. In 1976, the largest amount of meltwater issued from the south side and curved around the snout between the parking lot and the ice front, now far back from the little lake. The amount of water coming from the glacier varies greatly during the day as the amount of melting varies with the temperature and the amount of sunshine. It varies so much, in fact, that the meltwater lake visibly rises and falls each day in summer.

The mass of the Athabasca Glacier flows forward at about 15 metres per year. In the lower lobes, distinct flow-lines can be observed on the surface. Counterbalancing the forward flow of any glacier is the wastage of the ice, by melting and evaporation, and this is most effective near the foot of the glacier. The front edge of Athabasca Glacier has gone back about 30 metres a year for the last several years. This means that there is an actual wastage of 45 metres of ice from the front of the glacier.

The appearance of the edge of the glacier changes visibly from day to day in summer as large pieces spall off the ice-front, as new crevasses appear, and as melting proceeds. Photographs taken in 1950 and 1960 show quite different appearances from now, and photographs taken in 1920 show that the glacier extended hundreds of metres farther than at present. Climatic cycles are not entirely understood, so we cannot predict what is going to happen to the Athabasca Glacier and others like it in the Rockies. We do know, however, that melting exceeds supply at present, and although the Athabasca Glacier paused in its rate of recession in 1960-62, it seems likely that glaciers will continue to shrink for some time before the cycle swings to cooling and extension again.

Mount Edith Cavell

Mount Edith Cavell, at 3,365 metres (11,033 feet), is cut into Precambrian and Lower Cambrian rock beds that dip gently southwest. A great curving rock wall has been cut into the northeastern face of the mountain, and it is this side that provides the very beautiful view from the end of the road and from Jasper itself. Other views of this famous peak from farther south along the main highway at Leach Lake or beyond Athabasca Falls are less impressive and not as well known.

The mountain itself forms part of a long line of mountains ex-

The ridge leading from the foreground down the valley side to the Mount Edith Cavell tea room is a lateral moraine—that is, a mound of glacial debris heaped up along the side of a glacier that once occupied the valley.

tending for many kilometres along the southwest side of the Athabasca River valley. They were all sharply truncated by glaciers that formerly moved along the main valley system. Structurally, Mount Edith Cavell is also continuous with the mountains along the valley, for it lies on the southwest side of an *anticlinal* structure extending for many kilometres to the southeast. The rocks, of Lower Cambrian and Precambrian age, are almost entirely made of quartzite which comes from the recrystallization of sandstone.

Minor *scree* slopes all along the bottom of the cliffs send down a steady rain of fragments. Heavy accumulations of snow, along shelves and in protected places on the peak, melt in summer and occasionally fall in feathery slides over the dark rocky cliffs.

Angel Glacier lies in a saddle on the flank of Mount Edith Cavell and sends a tongue of ice over the edge of the cliff into the valley below. Pictures taken fifty years ago show it extending all the way to the valley bottom.

Angel Glacier lies in a saddle area on the northeast slope and sends a tongue of ice over the cliffside. In very recent times it reached continuously to the valley bottom but has been steadily shrinking so that it now hangs suspended on the rocky wall as a sort of immobilized icefall. Below it are large cones of debris mixed with ice, and a flush of meltwater issues from the bottom of the ice tongue in summer. A triangular area of rock more lightly stained than that around it suggests the former shape of Angel Glacier.

A walk into the bottom of the valley opposite the end of Angel Glacier takes you over a mass of boulders and cobbles, sand and rock flour, which has come directly from the grinding and wearing of the rocks all around by moving ice. In the lowest spot of the main amphitheatre is a small lake. The mass of rubble closer to the mountain and up the valley from it can be seen to be lying on a tongue of ice. If melting continues to exceed the supply of ice, this mass will gradually shrink and leave a basin that will fill with meltwater.

A view up and down the valley from just opposite Angel Glacier suggests that the whole valley was occupied by a much larger glacier—one to which the ancestral Angel Glacier was but a small tributary. *Lateral moraines*—piles of rock waste left along the sides of glaciers—occur along both sides of the valley above the end of the road and parking lot. Some of these are very steep sided towards the ice, and show clearly on their backs that they were pushed up against the banks there.

The first small ridges you climb over at the very edge of the parking lot are *terminal moraines*—piles of debris left along the front margins of glaciers. Down the valley a short distance and visible from the tops of the moraines just mentioned, lies a small lake which is held in by a dam of glacial debris that probably represents more terminal moraine material.

The water in the small brook that passes beside the parking lot comes from the drainage of the valley above. It includes the meltwater from the foot of Angel Glacier, the drainage from the valley extension to the southeast with its snowbanks, and the water coming from the melting of the residual ice below the till or debris. It is washing the finer particles out of the mixed debris and carrying it downstream to the upper end of the lake below, where it has already built a flat delta area complete with wandering distributaries.

Lakes of the Athabasca River Valley

Jasper Lake, 6 kilometres long and one and a half kilometres wide, lies in the course of the Athabasca River about 24 kilometres east of Jasper village. Beside it are several smaller lakes which have been cut off from it by drifting sand. Brûlé Lake is another large lake that lies in the course of the Athabasca River just east of the park boundary. All these and others near Jasper are remnants of meltwater that

This view of Mount Athabasca may be seen from the chalet or from the parking lot at the foot of the glacier. The fresher white snow on the upper slopes contrasts with the grey wrinkled masses of glacier ice draped over the rocks. The pattern changes rapidly in the lower reaches because the ice is thin there.

Pyramid Mountain dominates the view northward from Jasper. It is made of Lower Cambrian and Precambrian quartzites that weather to a reddish brown colour. In this view across Edith Lake, a tree-covered ridge of glacial deposits obscures Athabasca River, which lies between the lake and the mountain.

flooded the valley of the Athabasca River after the retreat of the main ice sheets to form a lake that was 96 kilometres long and stood as much as 107 metres above the present level of the river.

It seems likely that at the height of glaciation the valley of the Athabasca River carried the main flow of ice eastward off the mountains. Major tributaries came into it from the valleys now occupied by the Whirlpool River, Astoria River (near Mount Edith Cavell), Miette River, Maligne River and others. Enormous quantities of loose material and rock rubble were transported by the moving ice and deposited farther down. It was probably a mass of this debris that dammed up the old river valley so that a large lake was formed when the ice melted back from it. The dam was eventually cut through or around and the water level intermittently lowered. As the level of the old lake went down, deltas and terraces were formed at each of the different levels. Other temporary lakes were formed between the glacial ice and the sides of the valley.

An easily visible terrace of lake sands and gravels flanks the Jasper-Edmonton highway about 2 kilometres east of Jasper. Other views of this terrace, and others like it as high as 107 metres above present river levels, occur all along this highway down the Athabasca River to the east gate. The highway is along the top of one of them, northeast of the Palisade. The old road obviously cuts through the edge of it to the next level, about 2 kilometres east of the railway crossing near Henry House. Another place that several terraces may be seen is about 5 kilometres south of Jasper where the road passes from one to the next, in a series of steps. Here they are close to the present river level for they are higher up the river nearer the head of the old lake.

MT. L

GSC

Alpine meadows in exposed places, and patches of woods in more protected spots, characterize the passes in the Rocky Mountains at about two thousand metres above sea level. The boundary between Banff and Jasper parks lies near here at the summit of Sunwapta Pass.

The north side of Mount Athabasca displays a beautiful capping of snow with a thin drapery of crevassed ice flowing out from underneath onto the lower slopes. Melting in warm seasons quickly exposes larger areas of freshly scarred rock.

Opposite: Athabasca Glacier's icy tongue reaches down the valley from Columbia Icefield. In 1900 the glacier filled nearly all the foreground but by 1960 the ice stood as shown here. You can compare this picture with its present position to see the latest changes.

On the steep slope at the north end of Athabasca Glacier a meltwater stream comes swishing down in a most unusual serpentine pattern. You can see clearly how the fast-moving water piles up on the outsides of the bends so steeply that it falls back on itself. The clear glacial ice into which the stream is cutting contrasts with the granular dirt-covered surface.

A dam of bouldery debris collects
outwash sands and gravels in the
valley of the Sunwapta River about
five kilometres below Athabasca
Glacier. A scarred hillside above
suggests a landslide origin, but its
position in the valley suggests glacial
modification as well.

Opposite: A great rock glacier, a mass of boulders with some ice and water to lubricate it, flows very slowly down from the steep valley side to push a stream out of its course in this remote valley south of the highway, about twenty kilometres south of Sunwapta Pass.

This marvellous broken pyramid of limestone thrusts into the sky at the very head of Athabasca River in the southwestern corner of Jasper National Park.

Great glaciers pour off
the Continental Divide all
along the boundary
between Alberta and
British Columbia on the
western edges of Banff
and Jasper parks.

Mumm Peak dominates this view from Chetang Ridge down the valley of the Smoky River, not far from Robson Pass in the northwestern corner of Jasper National Park.

Below: Here, near the east gate on the Jasper-Edmonton highway, you see the upturned rocks of one of the series of ridges that form the eastern edge of the Rocky Mountains. In the foreground, the Athabasca River cuts across them just before it escapes eastward out onto the plains.

Opposite: Roche Miette dominates the roadside view like the prow of a great stone ship a few kilometres west of the east gate on the Edmonton-Jasper highway.

Below: Amethyst Lake and the Tonquin Valley lie in front of rugged peaks of the Continental Divide about twenty kilometres southwest of Jasper.

Opposite: The sheer face of Mount Edith Cavell, with its gently sloping snow-filled ledges and the mantle of glacial debris at its foot, is reflected serenely in the turquoise lake a kilometre or so below the end of the road.

Above: Pale green waters of the Maligne River
rush past great boulders between Maligne
Lake and Medicine Lake.

Right: One of the classical and most beautiful
views in the Canadian Rockies is this one in the
upper end of Maligne Lake.

Overleaf: After many kilometres of flowing underground, the waters of Maligne River issue forth along the bottom of a canyon seen here about half a kilometre below the tea room. Lichens and mineral stains colour the layered rocks that have been worn by the passing waters of an earlier time.

Roadlogs and Points of Interest

As you drive through Jasper National Park you pass a number of view-points, campspots, and other places where the view is especially good or where there are things of special geological interest. These are noted by number on the map facing page 64. What you can see at each of these places is described here.

Some people using this guide will be travelling upward in the numbered localities while others will be driving in the opposite direction, travelling downward in number from locality to locality. The approximate distance between adjacent stops is given between the sections describing them.

Travel in Jasper National Park is along three main routes: (1) the Banff-Jasper highway from Banff National Park at Sunwapta Pass, northwestward to Jasper; (2) the Edmonton-Jasper highway from the east gate to Jasper; and (3) Yellowhead Pass—Jasper road. The roadlogs which follow describe interesting spots along these routes as well as along the route from Jasper to the Maligne River valley, the Mount Edith Cavell side road, and the road to Miette Hot Springs. A trip from Jasper to the Palisade lookout tower is also described, and mention is made of other spots such as Tonquin Valley and Mount Robson.

Roadlog I
Sunwapta Pass to Jasper along the Banff-Jasper Highway

1 Sunwapta Pass

Jasper National Park and Banff National Park border one another along the divide between the headwaters of the North Saskatchewan River, which flows southeastward in this locality, and the headwaters of the Sunwapta River, which flows northwestward. The road crosses this divide in Sunwapta Pass at an elevation of about 2,035 metres (6,675 feet) above sea level. You will note that the forests are pretty thin at this elevation and that snowbanks are common in sheltered places and in places where the snow accumulates to great depths during the winter. The water flowing down the Banff side of the boundary flows thousands of kilometres across the plains to enter Hudson Bay. The water that flows north from this divide runs into the Sunwapta River, which joins the Athabasca River and eventually the Mackenzie river system, to empty at last into the Arctic Ocean.

The slopes of Nigel Peak rise from the valley to the east and northeast opposite this spot on the highway. The uppermost part of the peak is castellated with nearly vertical cliffs of limestone alternating with slopes of shaly rock, which together belong to the Rundle Formation of Mississippian age. Underneath it lies the Banff Formation, which weathers to form gentler slopes. The thick grey limestone in the bottom cliffs of Nigel Peak belongs to the Palliser Formation of Devonian age. This grey limestone unit is known up and down the length of the Rocky Mountains in great cliffs in the sides of mountains. Beneath it, but mostly hidden by the talus slope, lies the Fairholme Formation.

The rocks in Nigel Peak lie in the axial part of a downfold or *syncline* and are the youngest rocks to be seen from the highway between the southern boundary and Jasper. The downfold or syncline of which Nigel Peak is a part extends all the way southward through Banff Park to Mount Eisenhower and from the Banff-Jasper boundary northward 72 kilometres to Mount Kerkeslin. A view southeast along the valley from this spot shows another part of the same syncline clearly exposed in a mountain far to the south in Banff National Park.

Glimpses of the edges of the Columbia Icefield may be seen as a white rim on the mountains to the west and northwest. Immediately to the southwest lies Mount Athabasca which radiates glaciers in several directions. A view along the main highway westward shows the sharp

edge of Wilcox Peak just to the right of the valley.

Sunwapta Pass to Columbia Icefield chalet area — 4.5 kilometres (2.8 miles)

A tongue of Dome Glacier extends out underneath a stretch of rocky debris. The dark patches in the centre are where the surface debris has slumped down to reveal the ice itself.

2 Columbia Icefield Chalet Area

A superb view of mountains and glaciers is presented from the Columbia Icefield chalet area or, if you have an hour to walk up and back, from the hillside above and a little north of the chalet area. To the west and southwest a great tongue of ice, the Athabasca Glacier, issues from the Columbia Icefield over three great icefalls which appear like terraces at its back. To the left, a very sharp ridge stands high above the surface of the present ice. This represents an accumulation of debris that was scraped and pushed along the side of the Athabasca Glacier when it was much larger than it is now. Irregular mounds of debris in the foreground also tell of its once-greater extent. Access roads lead across the waste-cluttered valley bottom to the foot of the glacier and also to a lookoff point on the lateral moraine to the south of the glacier. A meltwater lake lies below the front of the glacier.

The Columbia Icefield can be seen rimming the mountains farther to the right. In the main valley to the right, Dome Glacier is formed by the refreezing together or reconstitution of ice and snow which fall over the cliff at the back of the valley. In the bottom of this valley a great mass of rock waste, tongues of ice, meltwater streams, and sharp-ridged lateral moraines can clearly be seen.

To the left of Athabasca Glacier, Mount Athabasca dominates the scene, and from its snowy shoulder it sends a glacier into a valley that is partly hidden by the shoulder of an intermediate mountain.

All the mountains in the view to the west and southwest are carved in sedimentary rocks of Cambrian age. The axial or central part of an upfold, or anticline, crosses the region about halfway back along the Athabasca Glacier valley and the Dome Glacier valley. Thus, at the backs of these valleys the rocks are dipping gently away from you and in the nearer parts of the valleys they are dipping gently towards you. The hills to the north and east of the chalet lie close to the centre or axial

part of a downfold or syncline. This relationship means that younger rocks appear in the hills back of the chalet and older rocks in the mountains across the valley.

What a scene this must have been when the whole valley was full of ice swinging down from the high country, across the front of where you stand to continue on down the valley to its melting.

Columbia Icefield chalet area to highway stop — about 3 kilometres (almost 2 miles)

3 Highway Stop
From this viewpoint on the bottom of the Sunwapta River valley, about 2.5 kilometres northwest of the Icefield Chalet, a number of features make it worth while to stop and look around. A superb scree or talus slope lies on the flank of Wilcox Peak to the northeast, and because it accumulates by the falling of debris from above, its boulders provide a complete sampling of the rocks in the upper parts of the mountain. The profile of Wilcox Peak shows a very steep wall on this side — the result of cutting by glaciers that filled the valley.

The valley bottom here and above it to the foot of the ice of Athabasca Glacier itself, is choked with glacial debris left there by the glaciers or washed into it by meltwaters in the time since they retreated. As you

Above: This view on the west side of Athabasca Glacier shows the heavy load of rock waste that tumbles onto the glacier from the cliffs, and the rush of meltwater pouring off it on a warm summer day. *Below:* The rock-strewn edge of the glacier is seen in a southward view from a shoulder of glacial debris.

look southeastward up the valley from this point, the snow-covered peak of Mount Athabasca dominates the skyline. The glacier which it sends down its northward face has several beautiful icefalls on it. It gives the impression of being a thin veneer of ice draped over the rounded rock surfaces, and this is confirmed in the lower regions where several *bosses* of rock show through the ice. To the southwest, the mountains which culminate in Mount Kitchener are cut in nearly horizontal Cambrian sedimentary rocks.

Highway stop to crest of hill—
3.2 kilometres (2.0 miles)

4   Crest of the Hill

From this point there is an excellent view up and down the valley of the Sunwapta River and of the mountains to the westward. Up the valley to the southeast, the tip of Athabasca Glacier, with a high wall of debris in its southern lateral moraine, lies beyond the gravel-filled upper valley of the Sunwapta River. Beyond that, Mount Athabasca shows three glaciers with icefalls, snowfields in their heads, and great cracks or *bergschrund* showing high up where the snow and ice have started to pull away from the steep back walls. In several places to the southwest, across the valley, the white rim of the Colum-bia Icefield shows on the skyline and through gaps in the mountains. The mountain directly opposite and to the southwest is Mount Kitchener. Farther west is a display of rugged peaks, including Diadem Peak with a mass of white ice on its right flank to the west or the right in this view. Stutfield Peak lies covered in ice just to the right of Mount Kitchener.

A view from the outside edge of the road shows the steep-walled gorge of the Sunwapta River cut in middle Cambrian limestones far below. It is interesting to note that above the canyon the river wanders around on a great mass of sand and gravel, and then cuts through a barrier before plunging into a rock-bound canyon below. The barrier seems to have a complicated story in it, for you will see that it is bedrock in its lowest parts, that above the bedrock is brownish glacial debris which may be a terminal moraine of the old glacier, and that on top it is clear that the grey limestone boulders have come from the broken cliffs above, either in a rockfall or by gradual accumulation, or both. It is possible, too, that there is another deep canyon buried under the present barrier and that the river has been forced into its present course by glacial damming. Below the barrier, the river once more wanders around on flats covered with sand and gravel in a network of interlacing channels.

Below this stop, a stream of clean silt-free water issues from under the scree slope and tumbles over the canyon wall into the brown silty water of the main river.

The rock-cuts, which line the road for several thousand metres on either side of this viewpoint, expose massive grey limestones of upper Cambrian and lower Ordovician age, with white calcite veins and joint facings. Farther up the slopes, younger Ordovician strata are exposed in Wilcox Peak, behind which lies the axial part of a syncline that runs up and down the whole length of the Athabasca-Sunwapta system. The very brown scree slope on the opposite side of the valley from here is cut into upper Cambrian rocks, as are the limestone cliffs just above it.

Crest of hill stop to Stutfield Glacier viewpoint—2.7 kilometres (1.7 miles)

5 Stutfield Glacier Viewpoint

Below and beside you at this point is a good example of a braided river flat—a valley bottom filled with sand and gravel with a river spread across it in interlacing channels. To the right and on the other side of the river, an *alluvial fan,* made of rock waste from the Stutfield Glacier and valley, spreads onto the valley flat. Opposite this point, glimpses of the Columbia Icefield can be seen along the edges of the mountains. A

superb double set of icefalls occurs on the steep back wall of Stutfield Glacier opposite you. Most of the main glacier in the bottom, made by reconstitution of broken ice below the icefalls, is hidden by the intervening wooded ridge. Mount Kitchener is to the left of Stutfield Glacier and shows the edge of the Columbia Icefield in cross section all along its crest, like the icing on a cake.

Just opposite and high on the shoulder of the mountain, a bowl-shaped depression or *cirque,* formed by glacial cutting, lies close enough to the edge so that its terminal moraine material has poured over the shoulder of the mountain to make a tall scree slope. Beside you and to the north is the brown-weathering upper Cambrian and lower Ordovician section on the flank of Tangle Ridge.

Stutfield Glacier viewpoint to site opposite old bridge at mouth of Beauty Creek—5.8 kilometres (3.6 miles)

6 Roadside Stop Opposite the Old Bridge at the Mouth of Beauty Creek

Beauty Creek is a fast-flowing mountain stream which rises in the valley behind Tangle Ridge, then falls precipitously to the level of the Sunwapta River. A short walk above the old bridge will show you a deep

The numerous scratches on the face of this boulder show that it has been caught up by moving glacier ice, tumbled against other boulders, and scraped over the hard rock bottom. The coin on the boulder gives the scale.

canyon cut in limestone, with numerous waterfalls, one after another.

To the east the mass of Tangle Ridge rises above you. The massive grey limestone in the base is of middle Cambrian age and the upper slopes are upper Cambrian and Ordovician rocks. One rock bed, well up· the mountain, makes a distinctive brownish scree slope and is topped by more massive, spiky, flat-lying limestone.

Southward, straight up the road, is a glimpse of the rim of the Columbia Icefield. Far to the northwest, along the main valley of the

This view from the southeastern shoulder of Wilcox Peak shows the rim of ice and snow of Columbia Icefield along the top of the cliffs and the place where it spills over to form Dome Glacier. On the left is the ridge of a lateral moraine.

Sunwapta River, the upturned edges of lower Cambrian and Precambrian quartzites form the Endless Chain Ridge.

You may note that the highway engineers have built groins along the road embankment to keep the river away from the highway. Some of these are filling with river-carried sediments, which further help the process. At this stop most of the sediments are fine silts and muds, the coarser fraction having been filtered out higher upstream. The river is said to be *braided* when it breaks up into innumerable channels which separate and rejoin over and over again as they do on this valley flat.

Site opposite old bridge at mouth of Beauty Creek to roadside stop on valley floor— 5.8 kilometres (3.6 miles)

7   Roadside Stop on Valley Floor

From this position on the valley floor, a view southeast up the valley of the Sunwapta River shows the end of Tangle Ridge with a spur of massive Cambrian limestone cutting off the far valley. Across the valley lies a mass of jagged peaks cut into thick-bedded, nearly flat, sedimentary rocks which lie close to the axis of the syncline or downfold passing all along this valley. The several peaks with glaciers and snow patches are in the Churchill Range with Diadem Peak and its spurs prominent to the left. On the northeast side of the valley (the left side as you look upstream), the rocks dip to the southwest towards the valley itself. All the rocks visible except for the top of Tangle Ridge are of Cambrian age.

A view to the northwest or down the Sunwapta River valley shows the great dip slopes of the lower Cambrian and Precambrian rocks of the Endless Chain Ridge. Outcropping rocks all along this section of the road in the valley bottom are of middle Cambrian limestone and dolomite formations near the bottom part of the downfold or syncline that underlies this valley.

Roadside stop on valley floor to landslide area between Poboktan Creek and Jonas Creek bridges— 7.6 kilometres (4.7 miles)

8   Landslide Area between Poboktan Creek and Jonas Creek Bridges

As you drive along the road, you suddenly enter a great boulder field with scattered trees and some small ponds. Glance up the slopes to the east (the right-hand side of the road as you face downriver) and you will see a great scar in the hillside, with more or less fresh pink rock surfaces exposed. It was from this scarred area that a vast quantity of rock let loose, cascaded down the slope of the mountain to swoop across the flat area where the road is now and on to the bottom of the river valley itself. The Sunwapta River now breaks in rapids over the foot of the slide area. The rock itself is quartzite of lower Cambrian age and has been used extensively for building stone in Jasper National Park.

Where the road crosses the slide, the freshly turned over boulders show that the rock itself is mostly light pink or buff. The slide area consists of rocks darkened with a covering of lichens, and if you observe carefully you will see some areas are darker than others. It would seem thus that there have been several slides in this area, and a glance up the hill shows several scar areas.

Off to the southeast, Sunwapta Peak and its subsidiary hills loom in the sky. These are fine examples of mountains cut into dipping sedimentary strata, with the dip slope facing the valley of the Sunwapta River and an irregular slope cut across the edges of the beds facing the valley of Jonas Creek. A view in

Between Jonas and Poboktan creeks, the Banff-Jasper highway passes through an old landslide. Beyond lies Sunwapta Peak.

the other direction shows the sweeping slopes of the Endless Chain Ridge stretching away off to the northwest.

Directly across the river from here, the steep slopes of the mountains are broken by a sharply marked glacial gorge which exposes in its flanks reddish orange quartzites of about the same kind as those in the landslide area.

Landslide area between Poboktan Creek and Jonas Creek bridges to roadside stop—12.0 kilometres (7.5 miles)

Sunwapta Peak rises 3,315 metres (10,875 feet) above sea level and is visible from several parts of the Banff-Jasper highway. In this aerial view, the rocks that underlie it and the adjacent peaks dip from left to right.

9 Roadside Stop

At this point you are close to the axial part of the syncline or downfold; that is, close to the very bottom of the trough of rocks that dip in from each side toward the centre. On the northeast side, great dip slopes of pink quartzites form the flanks of the Endless Chain Ridge. On the other side of the valley and on the other side of the trough or syncline, the crests of the mountains are in rocks that clearly dip toward you. One can almost feel hemmed in by the sides of this great downfold of the rocks.

A view southeast up the Sunwapta River valley shows the mass of Sunwapta Peak with its snowy banks and its satellites all cut into rocks dipping to the right or west. The peaks on the other side or right side of the valley dip in toward it, once again showing the synclinal or troughlike structure of the rocks. A view northwestward toward Jasper shows the long dip slopes of the Endless Chain Ridge stretching off into the distance and leading one's eye into the mass of Mount Kerkeslin. In the same direction but a little to the left, the tip of Mount Edith Cavell shows from nearly 40 kilometres away.

Roadside stop to Sunwapta Falls and canyon—8.4 kilometres (5.2 miles)

10 Sunwapta Falls and Canyon

A branch road about a kilometre long leads from the main Banff-Jasper highway to Sunwapta Falls and canyon. From the road junction the view northwest shows the bedding of the rocks to be nearly flat. Straight along the road but a little to the right, the beds dip conspicuously toward the valley bottom. Southeastward up the Sunwapta River valley, great dip slopes of lower Cambrian quartzites in the Endless Chain Ridge form the northeast side of the *syncline* or troughlike fold whose axis runs along the valley of the river. Very prominent on the right side of the valley is Gong Mountain, which also dips conspicuously inward toward the centre of the fold in the river valley.

At the falls itself we find a place where the Sunwapta River changes course sharply from northwest to southwest and then plunges over the falls into a deep canyon. It seems likely that the river has been pushed out of a preglacial valley by glacial damming. The falls resulted when the river flowed over the edge of ready-made cliffs, and since then it has gradually worked its way back by erosion to form the canyon.

Just below the footbridge the canyon takes an abrupt right-angle bend, indicating that a fault or joint system in the rock may partly control the direction of river erosion. The rocks at the falls and in the upper part of the canyon dip very

93

Here Sunwapta River changes its course from northwest to southwest and plunges over Sunwapta Falls. Two kilometres farther on it joins Athabasca River on the valley flat.

Sunwapta Falls and canyon to Athabasca Valley viewpoint and Honeymoon Lake area — 4.2 kilometres (2.6 miles)

gently, for this region is very close to the bottom of the trough or synclinal fold in the area.

After about two kilometres of turbulent flow and other falls, the Sunwapta River reaches the valley flat of the Athabasca River, which comes from the south and joins it a little farther on.

11 Athabasca Valley Viewpoint and Honeymoon Lake Area

From the crest of the hill just above the Honeymoon Lake turnoff the syncline in the Sunwapta River valley is clearly visible in Gong Mountain on the right and the beautiful dip slopes of the Endless Chain Ridge on the left. To the northwest lies the mass of Mount Kerkeslin which includes the centre and some of each side of the syncline so that the mountain itself shows quite clearly the downfold or synclinal structure. Off to the northwest is a sharp conical mountain standing above the general high mass. This is an unusual view of Mount Edith Cavell.

An especially impressive view of the Endless Chain Ridge may be had from the shore of Honeymoon Lake and the campsite there. One huge boulder of pebbly quartzite stands by itself beside the enclosure at Honeymoon Lake campsite.

From the Athabasca Valley viewpoint is one of the great views of the Rocky Mountains at their best. As you face the valley, a collection of ragged points and peaks opposite culminates in Dragon Peak; and back out of sight, is ice-covered Catacomb Peak at 3,294 metres (10,800 feet) above sea level. You can see the dark colour and unusual texture on the surface of the ancient Precambrian quartzites in this mass. To its left, the valley of the Athabasca sweeps away to the southward to the great peaks and spikes of the Continental Divide, which is also the boundary between Alberta and British Columbia. The highest peak is Mount Columbia at 3,749 metres (12,294 feet). The Banff-Jasper highway follows the valley of the Sunwapta River to the

left of the mountain mass, dominated by Gong Mountain, on that side of the Athabasca Valley.

A little to the right of opposite you is Mount Christie at 3,105 metres (10,180 feet) and from here you can see a small glacier cradled in its pouchlike cirque on the mountain front. Brussels Peak projects from the ridge leading back from Mount Christie like some great ship's funnel. You can see that the rocks in the front of this mountain mass are the same as those in Dragon Peak but that the upper parts are in younger rocks lying above them. Farther to the right is Mount Fryatt at 3,363 metres (11,026 feet) the highest peak nearby, in still younger rocks that make its strangely shaped head with the flat hat that slopes towards you. Its highest point reaches far enough up into the rock section to include Ordovician rocks. It is clear from the view of the rocks along this front and from glimpses of peaks and valleys beyond it that we are looking at the edge of a syncline or downfold, with the rocks dipping away from us, and that it extends for many kilometres to the north.

Back of here is a series of ridges that are part of another syncline clearly visible in the back of Mount Kerkeslin, the end of the ridge just to the right of the road looking northward towards Jasper. This means that the Athabasca River valley in this area lies in the corresponding upfold or anticline between the two synclines.

The banks of the road here are cut into glacial deposits of fairly well rounded boulders in a fine matrix of sand, silt and clay. Below the road in this locality, the Athabasca River, which has received a very large tributary, the Sunwapta River, is a stream of considerable size and it flows sedately on a flat, wooded, valley bottom.

Athabasca Valley viewpoint to stop beside the Athabasca River—7.2 kilometres (4.5 miles)

12 Roadside Stop beside the Athabasca River

Right beside the Athabasca River you can feel the processes of erosion that have shaped the magnificent scenery of this whole area, when you hear the rushing sounds of one of them—the river—and see right before you the silt-laden waters on their way to the distant sea. Look at the fine silts that are exposed on the ends of the small islands, and observe the ripple marks.

Towards Banff, or left as you face the river, the long serrated ridge is the Endless Chain, made of ancient pink and white quartzites, dipping down and to the right. Just above the trees in the middle of the valley, rocks are seen to be dipping to the left, showing clearly the great syn-cline or downfold that the highway follows for many kilometres. The central portion of the same syncline is preserved in the ridge behind you, which ends on its north face in a perfect cross section on the face of Mount Kerkeslin.

Across the valley is the peak of Mount Christie capping a block of old Precambrian rocks that dip away from you, as you can see all along the mountain front to the right. The strange little peak visible in the saddle is Mount Fryatt at 3,363 metres (11,026 feet), the highest peak around, and unusual because it preserves a small portion of the centre of the syncline on the far side of the river. Be on the lookout along this section for other glimpses of this fold structure in the mountains and valleys cut into it. The rocks behind this stopping place are part of the Kerkeslin syncline and are clearly not standing on their edges as those in Endless Chain do.

Roadside stop to viewpoint (Goat Lick)—3.0 kilometres (1.9 miles)

13 Viewpoint on Southwest Side of the Road (Goat Lick)

One can see for many kilometres up and down the wooded Athabasca River valley with the full spread of the high mountains on the other side. Immediately below you, the Athabasca River flows swiftly but not violently on its way, forming is-

Above: Precambrian quartzites form the Endless Chain Ridge.
Below: The flat-bottomed valley of Athabasca River contrasts with the great rock walls carved by glaciers long ago. In this view from the overlook south of Athabasca Falls, Mount Christie is seen with Brussels Peak behind it.

lands in some places, cutting into banks and leaving deposits on others. Its origin in glacial meltwaters is clearly seen in the colour of its silt-laden waters.

The bank on which the viewpoint is situated is made up largely of very finely ground-up rock flour that had its origin in glacial action. It is overlain by layers of coarser gravels which constantly fall down over the finer material as it is undercut by the river below. This is a favourite haunt of goats and other animals looking for salt licks.

The mountains opposite are cut into a great thickness of Precambrian and Cambrian quartzite that grades upward into limestone. Opposite you, the highest peak is Mount Fryatt, 3,363 metres (11,026 feet), which is easily recognized by its peculiar sloping peak. At certain times of day, the lower Ordovician limestone at its very top appears to be buff. Farther to the left and almost due south of the viewpoint lies Mount Christie, with small glaciers on its front and a steep valley that seems to be cut into it just below the peak. Behind Mount Christie on the same ridge lies the steep-walled Brussels Peak, looking rather like the funnel of a large ship, and behind that again is a third peak, Mount Lowell.

To the northeast of this viewpoint, directly behind as you face the river, Mount Kerkeslin rises to nearly 2,987 metres (9,800 feet) and shows orange-red and red-stained cliffs of Precambrian and lower Cambrian quartzites. From here Mount Kerkeslin no longer appears to be in the bottom part of a trough structure for you are looking at the edge of the fold instead of the cross section.

Viewpoint to junction of Routes 93 and 93A — 5.8 kilometres (3.6 miles)

14 Parking Area just above Road Junction, and Athabasca Falls

From here a superb view spreads to the south and west. The great bulk of Whirlpool Mountain looms directly to the southwest. Southeastward (left), several mountain masses of smaller magnitude are climaxed by Mount Fryatt, which from this viewpoint is clearly synclinal or of troughlike structure. Still farther to the left, Mount Christie, with Brussels Peak behind it and Mount Lowell the third peak on that ridge, continues the mountain front along the southwest side of the Athabasca River valley to Dragon Peak where the view is cut off by the shoulder of nearby Mount Kerkeslin. These mountains are carved largely in Cambrian quartzite which gives way upward to Cambrian limestones. Mount Fryatt penetrates upwards in the section far enough to include some Ordovician rocks at its peak.

To the right of Whirlpool Mountain, the valley of the Whirlpool River leads away to the southwest with numerous high peaks in the distance. The sharp peak on top of a rugged plateau to the west, more to the right through the screen of trees, is Mount Edith Cavell in a view quite unlike the one that is ordinarily pictured. Directly opposite, several *cirques* or glacially cut, bowllike depressions occur along the mountain front. One has a little glacier in it still and you can see the darker, grey green, old ice with rem-

At the foot of Mount Kerkeslin the Athabasca River plunges over a cliff of Precambrian quartzites into a narrow canyon of its own cutting. The fine sediment suspended in the water gives it its milky appearance.

nants of last year's snow on it. One to the left has a waterfall at the back, and you can wonder whether there is a little gem of a *tarn* or glacial lake cradled in it behind the treed rim.

Across the front of the view swiftly flows the Athabasca River with its constant roar and standing waves. Just a few hundred metres

Right: The whole volume of the Athabasca River pours through the narrow gorge in the centre of this photograph. It was over these cliffs that the river originally cascaded, but erosion has gradually moved the falls upstream to their present position.

Below: This view of the gorge is from the bridge at the Athabasca Falls. The weathering of the quartzites in the lower gorge has etched out the bedding planes.

farther on, it quickens and plunges over a ragged cliff of Precambrian quartzite in Athabasca Falls. Below the falls the river flows swiftly down a narrow gorge of its own cutting and emerges at a line of cliffs a few hundred metres beyond. Near the falls and in the woods along the left bank (always as you face down stream), abundant channels and old potholes show that the river once flowed over a broad section of the rocky cliffs. The present falls will slowly cut more deeply into the central section of the river bed and abandon the flatter side areas which were more broadly flooded as little as fifteen years ago.

High above in the background looms Mount Kerkeslin with its gently down-bowed sedimentary rocks. Wooded slopes reach partly up its flanks, giving way there to bare scree or talus. Above this the Precambrian and Cambrian quartzites lie layer upon layer to the very peak. You may notice two bright red layers in the lower part of the cliff just above the tree line on the left or northwest face of Mount Kerkeslin. These contain abundant iron oxide or hematite which gives them their colour. Look at the pattern of gullies and ridges in the southwest face of Kerkeslin with occasional slide areas extending down into the woods.

Junction of 93 and 93A to two viewpoints—6.8 kilometres (4.2 miles)

15 Two Viewpoints on Highway Curve

Two viewing areas about half a kilometre apart are located on a sweeping curve in the highway. The view is about the same. Directly to the south, Mount Kerkeslin thrusts its synclinal mass of rocks some 2,987 metres (9,800 feet) above sea level and gives way to the left or east to the evenly dipping, rusty rocks of Mount Hardisty. Below, you can hear the Athabasca as it carries its load of glacial silt and fine muds northward towards the sea.

Away to the west, Mount Edith Cavell, with its half-pyramid peak with snow on the right side, caps a large mass of Precambrian and Cambrian quartzites. To the right or northward of Edith Cavell, a line of hills occupies the skyline to the conspicuous break of the valley of Miette River along which the Yellowhead Pass road is routed. Far to the right, the mass of Pyramid Mountain and adjacent mountains directly north of Jasper is cut into Precambrian quartzites that in many lights have a distinctive dark red appearance. To the left of Edith Cavell the gap made by the valley of Whirlpool River allows us to see many distant peaks near the Continental Divide and the Alberta—British Columbia boundary far southwestward. To the left or southeast of the Whirlpool River valley, the mass of Whirlpool Mountain is

Shadows of clouds move over the slopes of Whirlpool Mountain. This mass of sedimentary rocks of Precambrian and Cambrian age lies at the junction of the Whirlpool and Athabasca rivers.

the beginning of a long line of mountains extending to the south-east through the distinctive sloping peak of Mount Fryatt, to Mount Christie and its vertical-walled satellite (Brussels Peak) behind it, and Mount Lowell the third in the same ridge.

Horseshoe Lake, a lovely, clear, rock-bound lake, lies in a deep basin about a kilometre to the south on the east side of the road.

Viewpoint on highway curve to long rock-cut—2.6 kilometres (1.6 miles)

16 Road-cut
Long cuts along the road show a variety of Precambrian rocks typical of this area. Several different kinds of quartzite, slaty quartzite, micaceous quartzite, and dark slate

are visible. In some places the rock is folded into shapes that look like ripple marks. Tiny faults break the rock along the troughs of the folds.

Mount Hardisty, with its dark reddish brown quartzite slopes, looms to the south. There is a superb view of Mount Hardisty and Mount Kerkeslin from the long hill about half a kilometre to the north of here.

Road-cut to middle of river flat—
5.2 kilometres (3.1 miles)

17 River Flat
For several kilometres along here in each direction the road is on a river flat, developed on sand and bouldery gravel laid down by the Athabasca River and its ancestors. The highly rounded boulders and pebbles show long-continued water transportation. It seems most likely that this mass of material is mainly glacial debris, picked up and transported by the running river-water at a time when the Athabasca River stood higher than it does now. Nearby, the turbid waters of the Athabasca flow northward toward the sea, carrying enormous quantities of fine silt and suspended material that have come mostly from the grinding of the rocks by glaciers in the river's headwaters.

Southward, Mount Hardisty and its long gentle dip slopes of dark reddish brown quartzite is a companion to Mount Kerkeslin on its right with its downfolded or synclinal layers of Precambrian quartzite. The tip of Mount Edith Cavell peeks out above the long wooded slope leading northward from the northern end of this stop.

Middle of river flat to hilltop with river below and rock-cut—2.2 kilometres 1.4 miles

18 Hilltop and Rock-cut
From the south side of the hill on which this stop is situated, the whole circle of mountains to the south is beautifully shown. To the left, the gentle dip slopes of reddish brown quartzite of Mount Hardisty give way to its companion, Mount Kerkeslin, whose trough of downfolded quartzite is clearly visible in its northern shoulder. Farther to the right and many kilometres beyond, the line of mountains between Whirlpool Mountain and the Sunwapta River junction is dominated by Mount Christie's sharp peak and its steep-walled satellite, Brussels Peak. To the west and southwest, heavily wooded slopes lead to Mount Edith Cavell, although the famous peak itself is hidden from sight. Irregular mountains are in view to the northward as far as the Whistlers, on part of which is the cable car terminus. The Yellowhead Pass route is along the valley below and beyond.

Below the south face of the hill, the Athabasca River is cutting into a bank of yellow-grey glacial outwash with lots of very fine claylike material in it. On the south slope of the hill, rock-cuts expose grey and white quartzite. In one place, near the south end of the cuts, glacial scratches or *striae* are well preserved on the dense tough rock.

From the north slope of the same hill, the view is more open to the north. Tekarra's long ridge ends in a bold north-facing cliff, and the more rounded slopes of Signal Mountain lie below it. The mass of hills northwest of Jasper frames the valley of the Miette River and the rounded profile of the Whistlers to the south.

Hilltop to great sweeping curve in road—5.0 kilometres (3.1 miles)

19 Bend

From this position on the river flat, the view is partly hemmed in by the trees and nearby low hills. Far to the southeast some of Mount Kerkeslin may be seen through the trees, and beyond it, straight down the road, the range of mountains is dominated by Mount Christie's peak. Due south, the wooded slopes of Mount Edith Cavell frame the snowy top of the peak itself. Westward, the mass of mountains is broken by the valley of Portal Creek, a main route westward into

the valleys beyond, with the steep Peven Peak framed in it. Northward from here, the hills extend to the Miette River valley, along which the road to the Yellowhead Pass is routed. The mass of mountains northwest and north of Jasper is dominated by the dark, reddish mass of Pyramid Mountain. Its conspicuous layerings set it apart from the adjacent mountains.

Road-bend viewpoint to Athabasca River bridge—2.1 kilometres (1.3 miles)

20 Athabasca River Bridge

The bridge over the Athabasca River provides an open view in many directions. Southeastward up the river, the Precambrian quartzites of Mount Hardisty dip from the peak down into the right in gentle, dark red slopes. To its right, Mount Kerkeslin looms high in the sky with its downfolded trough of younger Precambrian rocks. Thirty-two kilometres to the southeast and a little to the right of the river valley, some peaks of a long line of mountains between the Sunwapta junction and the Whirlpool Valley are high enough to be seen from this distance. Due south of this point the mass of Edith Cavell is seen to be made up of sloping, layered rocks, emphasized by the way the snow follows the layering. To the north, beyond Jasper, a mass

Mount Kerkeslin's synclinal structure is clearly visible and below it the white scar of the highway, seen here from the flanks of Mount Edith Cavell fifteen kilometres away.

of mountains is dominated by Pyramid Mountain, with its reddish Precambrian quartzites. Immediately to the east, the ramparts of Mount Tekarra terminate a long ridge in a northwest-facing cliff, with the more rounded slopes of Signal Mountain below it to the northwest.

The silt-laden waters of the Athabasca River flow swiftly northeastward in the neighbourhood of the bridge. Where roadbuilding has disturbed the gravel along its banks, you may see how very rounded the cobbles and boulders are. Such rounding results from their being transported by water. The variety of rocks among the boulders and the variety of sizes of material indicate, on the other hand, a glacial origin. The great bulk of these deposits probably came from glacial outwash—glacial debris carried by moving ice and then fed to fast-flowing meltwater streams which eventually deposited it where it is now. In the river itself you may see elliptical islands of material that even now are in transit downstream.

Athabasca River bridge to junction of 93 and 93A—0.8 kilometre (0.5 mile) From junction of 93 and 93A to junction of 93 and 16—6.7 kilometres (4.2 miles)

21 *Jasper Village*
Twenty thousand years ago the site of Jasper was the junction of two great glaciers—one moving easterly down the valley now occupied by the Miette River, the Yellowhead Pass road and main line of the Canadian National Railways; the other moving northward in the valley now occupied by the Athabasca River and the Banff-Jasper highway. As the climate gradually warmed and the glaciers melted back, vast quantities of sand and gravel were deposited on the valley flat. The town of Jasper is built on these sands and gravels.

Northward from Jasper, the dark reddish mass of Pyramid Mountain, marked by runnels and slides and a tiny communications tower on top, dominates the scene. On its northeastern flank (to the right) the dark wooded slopes of the Palisade contrast sharply. To the east, the sharp peaks of Colin Range make a jagged skyline on the far side of the Athabasca River valley. There, the great limestone masses are standing on edge and the erosion of gullies across the general trend of the range makes the sawtooth-like outline of the individual peaks. Directly opposite Jasper, to the east, the rounded slopes of the Maligne Range give way to the bare top of Signal Mountain with the lookout station and farther away the rock ramparts of Mount Tekarra.

Straight south and up the Athabasca River valley the beautiful peak of Mount Edith Cavell, with its gently inclined layering of snow and rock, is an impressive view, particularly in the late afternoon sun. Rounded hills to the southwest include the Whistlers, closest at hand, and other peaks leading away southward toward Mount Edith Cavell.

In front of the town, the Athabasca River flows northward with its great load of finely divided sedimentary materials, on its way to the distant Arctic sea. Just south of the town the clear waters of the Miette River join the Athabasca and maintain their identity along the left bank for a hundred metres before becoming lost in the main grey stream.

The region around Jasper is dotted with lakes. Some of them, such as Beauvert, Annette, and Edith, lie on the river flat and are shrunken remnants of a very large lake that once filled the whole Athabasca River valley for many kilometres. Others, like Pyramid, Patricia, and a great number of smaller ones to the west of Jasper, have been formed by the glacial damming of valleys and hollows.

From junction of 93 and 16 to overlook and parking place on Highway 16 — 2.1 kilometres (1.3 miles)

22 Overlook and Parking Place about Halfway around Jasper By-pass on Highway 16

This viewpoint on a flat gravel terrace provides an open view of the Athabasca Valley all around. The river below is almost braided with its numerous islands and bars made of the debris of mountains being carried downstream.

Peeking out of the woods opposite and on this side of the river are many terraces and banks of glacial debris. These show how enormous the mighty glacier was at its height as it filled the whole valley, damming up lakes along its sides and spewing out great quantities of rocky debris in its melting. Each of the terrace levels reflects an old lake level.

Across the Athabasca Valley we see the wooded slopes of Signal Mountain leading to a minor rocky top and Mount Tekarra farther along the ridge. This ridge marks the northern end of the Maligne Mountains, which are formed of Precambrian quartzites and argillites but may also include some lower Cambrian rocks. These mountains are structurally continuous with Pyramid Mountain, which looms in the sky as a bare red-brown and dark grey, tent-shaped peak to the northwest with its communications tower on top. The Maligne Range, Pyramid Mountain, and those to the northwest, lie on the upper side of a great west-dipping fault or break in the earth's crust, along which these ancient rocks have ridden northeastward up and over younger rocks (see page 35).

The serrated peaks of the Colin Range form the skyline downstream to the northeast. Note how the vegetation follows the rock layers, being able to grow in some but not others because of the footing and the supply of water. The very much rounded outlines of the ski hills of the Whistlers complex are to the south, and the end of the hoist is prominent on one.

Mount Edith Cavell thrusts its readily recognized peak with its snowy inclined layers above the complex of mountains to the southeast. Right upstream is Kerkeslin's snowy front, with its snow-outlined synclinal structure very evident.

And as you have paused here, the river below has carried another few tons of rock waste towards the distant sea.

Roadlog II
East Gate to Jasper, on Edmonton-Jasper Highway

23   East Gate on Edmonton-Jasper Highway

The eastern boundary of Jasper National Park on the Edmonton-Jasper highway lies along a line that is the boundary between the Rocky Mountains and the Foothills to the east. From the gate area one can sense this in the different views to the east and to the west.

Southeast of the gate area, Roche à Perdrix shows the strongly folded rocks which are characteristic of the Front Ranges of the Rocky Mountains. An excellent example of a downfold or syncline is preserved in the larger left peak, with a complicated zone of folding in the centre and a long dip slope in the subsidiary peak to the right. To the southwest, or a little left of the road looking towards Jasper, the mass of Roche Miette and Miette Range loom over a wooded limestone ridge.

East gate on Edmonton-Jasper highway to bridge over Fiddle River— 1.6 kilometres (1.0 mile)

24   Bridge Crossing Fiddle River

The Fiddle River flows generally parallel to the northwest-trending mountain ridges, but a kilometre or so above this bridge it cuts directly across the lower Devonian rocks of Ashlar Ridge in a steep-walled canyon. The superb view across the Athabasca River shows the sloping beds and the fold structures as the cross-cutting valley reveals the inside secrets of the mountains. The boundary of Jasper National Park lies along the top of the first great ridge so that the green slopes on the right (east) are outside the park and all the mass of rocks to the left (west) from the first crest are in it. The same structural revelation is to be seen on this side of the valley, but the road is so close that the trees and nearer slopes most commonly obscure it. Note how the engineers have guided the channel of the Fiddle River by banks of boulders to prevent the usual spreading out as it reaches the Athabasca River grade.

Fiddle River bridge to roadside stop beside small lake—4.8 kilometres (3.0 miles)

25 Roadside Stop beside Small Lake

Above and across the lake is the vertical front of Roche Miette with a downfold structure on its left. Straight along the road towards Jasper, the high peaks and ridges are of the de Smet Range and, far beyond, the Victoria Cross Range. Opposite is the valley of Moosehorn

Creek with the Bosche Range to the left and the Boule Range to the right. Great sweeps and folds in the rocks are clearly visible. The rocks in all these ridges consist of Devonian and Carboniferous sedimentary units, which have been thrust up over the much younger Cretaceous beds during the folding and faulting of the Rocky Mountain System. This accounts for the complicated structures and also for the way in which older rocks lie on top of younger ones in apparent contradiction of the law of superposition (see p. 20).

Roadside stop beside small lake to junction with branch road to Miette Hot Springs—0.8 kilometre (0.5 mile) Along branch road to Punchbowl Falls—1.3 kilometres (0.8 mile)

26 Punchbowl Falls

Mountain Creek drops over the edge of a steeply dipping bed of conglomerate of Cretaceous age. Erosion of the overlying beds on the west side has formed a steep-walled valley into which the brook now tumbles. The unusual shape of Punchbowl Falls is due to a combination of things—the steepness of the dip of the conglomerate, the joints and irregularities in the conglomerate, and the way that water tends to fall straight down after it comes over the lip or edge of a cliff.

It appears likely that the first falls

Punchbowl Falls is on a small brook that crosses the road to Miette Hot Springs just over a kilometre from its junction with the main road at Pocahontas. The falls lie in a resistant conglomerate layer in a sequence of softer rocks.

here came over the edge of the conglomerate layer, arched through the
air, and then dropped vertically to
impinge on the cliff part way down.
This process gradually resulted in
the cutting of a depression at the
point of impact. As the depression
increased in size, a pool of turbulent
water began to form in it and to spill
out over the edge and thus start the
same process lower down. Mean-
while the upper lip of the falls was
gradually being etched back along
slight irregularities in the rock.

Roche Miette is formed of folded
Devonian rocks capped by Palliser
limestones. With a height of 2,316
metres (7,599 feet), it is a
conspicuous landmark to the
northeast of Jasper.

Remnants of former positions of
the falls may be seen along the side
and in front of the present cascade.

A seam of coal of low purity about
30 centimetres thick crops out at the
back of the lower lookout at
Punchbowl Falls.

Beds of rounded and sorted gravel

111

and sand form the side of the highway in several places near the falls. These were formed when meltwater streams picked up debris from the glaciers in the region, carried it a short distance, and then deposited it in rudely stratified banks.

The steep-walled peak of Roche Miette lies straight south of this stop and is visible from several places along the highway. The grey cliff area at the top consists of the Palliser Formation, well known throughout the Rockies as a rock unit that forms great grey cliffs. Small patches of younger rocks occur in structural basins here and there on the flanks of Roche Miette. The complex of folded rocks beneath the cliffs of the Palliser limestones are, for the most part, younger Devonian rocks.

Between Roche Miette and where you stand lies the trace of a great break in the solid rocks. Along this irregular surface the older rocks of the Roche Miette mass have been thrust up and over the younger rocks in the valley before you by enormous compressive stresses inside the fabric of the earth. Thus, the older Devonian and Carboniferous rocks in the mountain of Roche Miette are now above the younger Cretaceous rocks which underlie the valley before you.

Punchbowl Falls to viewpoint overlooking Fiddle River—
7.4 kilometres (4.6 miles)

27   *Viewpoint Overlooking Fiddle River*

The Miette Hot Springs road goes along the upturned edges of Cretaceous rock formations to this viewpoint. From here, the sedimentary units in the area can clearly be seen to be dipping downwards and to the southwest. Fiddle River, below, is cut in rocks of Triassic age. The skyline is formed in nearly vertical limestones of the Palliser Formation—that resistant rock unit found in so many cliffs and mountain tops. The spectacular sawtooth ridges on the slopes of Ashlar Ridge, with the vegetation following certain layers but not others and looking like a sergeant's stripes, are cut into the brown-weathering Banff Formation and the greyish Rundle Formation of Mississippian age. Although these sawtooth features are not isolated as individual mountains, you may wish to compare them with those on page 39.

Downstream, you can see the beginnings of the steep gorge where Fiddle River cuts across the trend of Ashlar Ridge. Toward the south and west, the complicated rock structures of the Miette Range form the skyline. On the way down the hill, contrast the thin-bedded rotten shales with the massive limestone in the enormous wall opposite.

Viewpoint overlooking Fiddle River to Miette Hot Springs—8.7 kilometres.
(5.4 miles)

28 Miette Hot Springs

The Miette Hot Springs form part of a chain of hot springs which appear here and there all along the Rocky Mountain System. They have been described in some detail on page 49.

Miette Hot Springs are in the steep valley of Sulphur Creek, presumably named because of the sulphurous content of the water added to the creek by the hot springs themselves.

Northward from here, part of the great wall of Ashlar Ridge and, beyond, part of Fiddle Range may be seen through the gap. To the south, Utopia Mountain rises some 2,560 metres (8,400 feet) above sea level and forms part of the general Miette-Nikanassin mountain range.

A sharp fold in the rocks just above and southeast of the village reminds us of the complicated rock structures beneath the surface.

From Miette Hot Springs back to junction with Edmonton-Jasper highway — 17.5 kilometres (10.9 miles)

Along highway to roadside stop near riverbank — 0.6 kilometre (0.4 mile)

29 Roadside Stop near Riverbank just Southwest of Warden's Station

The open view across the valley of the Athabasca River toward the northwest shows the comparatively flat valley of Moosehorn Creek between Bedson Ridge to the right and Bosche Range to the left. This comparatively flat low area extends across to this side of the river to include the Pocahontas district and the area where you are standing. The rocks that underlie it are of Cretaceous age and, therefore, comparatively young in the rock sequence of this district. They are especially interesting in that they contain seams of coal that supported a flourishing mining industry between 1911 and 1921. Remnants of the abandoned operations can still be seen around Pocahontas, and the piles of dark slack near this stop came from the old mines.

The structure of the mountains in this area is rather like shingles on a roof. Westward-dipping faults were planes of movement along which great slices of rock, thousands of metres thick, were pushed up, slice upon slice. Each of the ridges visible from here consists of the upthrust older rocks, and each of the valleys is underlain by younger rocks which have been overridden.

The great grey, snow-streaked wall of limestone of the de Smet Range may be seen to the west. Roche Miette stands ruggedly at the end of Miette Range to the south and southeast. Along the road in this neighbourhood, small dunes of wind-blown silt and fine sand derived from the exposed river flats remind us of the ever-present processes of erosion.

The complicated structures of the mountains of the Front Ranges may be seen here in the valley of the Athabasca River, directly opposite Disaster Point. Palliser limestone of Devonian age forms the light patch in Roche à Bosche at right, and also forms the great arch, or anticline, at centre.

*Roadside stop near riverbank to
roadside stop and parking area —
5.1 kilometres (3.2 miles)*

30 Roadside Stop in Parking Area Opposite Rock-cut

The face of the rock-cut has an interesting pattern made by the joints in the limestone dipping down and to the left, and by the drillholes used to blast it dipping down and to the right. Above the rock a few centimetres of wind-blown glacial silts give way upward to a dark organic top soil.

A superb exposure of folded and faulted rocks is visible across the river from this point. Opposite and to the left, the de Smet Range shows the upturned edges of a westward-dipping section of Devonian rocks, capped by the Palliser limestone. The near slopes are filigreed with snow-filled gullies cut across the upturned edges of the rock beds. A little farther to the right, a low partly wooded ridge shows a perfect example of an upfold or anticlinal structure. Carboniferous sedimentary units dip away on each side from the ever-present Palliser limestone which forms the grey mass at the centre. To its left is another S-shaped fold, as clearly seen in the left edge of the photo on page 114.

A series of ridges extends away from the right-hand slope of the anticlinal ridge just described. The nearest is Roche à Bosche, whose crest line is cut into the Palliser Formation. The wooded valley between Roche à Bosche and Roche Ronde to its right is underlain by the softer rocks of the Banff Formation of Mississippian age. The peak of Roche Ronde is in the grey Palliser limestones which also extend down the partly bare shoulder toward the river. In the distance upriver, the peak of well-named Pyramid Mountain with its snowy flank is capped with a communications tower and dominates the irregular mountains there.

This mixed-up arrangement of older and younger rocks is only possible in a folded sequence that has been faulted and broken along surfaces on which movement of one block upward over another has taken place. It gives one a feeling of awe to realize that these rocks were laid down long ago as flat-lying layers on the bottom of calm seas that once covered this region; and that since then they have been thrust up, folded and broken, and then deeply eroded over millions of years to produce the complicated pattern you can see here now.

And quietly rolls the Athabasca towards the distant sea.

*Roadside stop to Jasper House historic
site — 3.4 kilometres (2.1 miles)*

31 Jasper House Historic Site

The Athabasca River cuts almost

The southeastern end of Bosche Range shows spectacular rock structures. Here you can see the grey Palliser limestones in the peak of Roche Ronde (to the right) and in Roche à Bosche (centre). In between the peaks lie Banff Formation rocks.

---

directly across the northwest-trending mountain ranges here and provides a fairly easy access route across otherwise very difficult country. For this reason it has long been used by travellers including many of the early explorers and the Indians before them.

Away to the southwest stands the symmetrical snowy peak of Pyramid Mountain, just northwest of Jasper. To the southwest, on the same side of the river, is the Jacques Range and its extension to the northwest, the de Smet Range. The great, light grey mass of limestone in Roche Miette stands at the end of Miette Range along the skyline with patches of brown shales below grey limestone. Vegetation follows some layers up and down the serrated slopes. Its continuation can be seen across the river in Bosche Range.

Jasper House historic site to roadside stop near dunes—about 6.4 kilometres (4 miles)

32 Roadside Stop near Dunes

The very flat bottom of the Athabasca River valley in this area is the bottom of a lake that occupied the whole of this part of the Athabasca River basin in postglacial times. Jasper Lake, in the course of the Athabasca River, is a tiny remnant of it. The dunes and piles of wind-blown sand along this section of the road and to the south of it are

Mount Greenock is seen here across the still waters of the upper end of Jasper Lake. It is made up of a mass of Devonian and Carboniferous rocks which have been thrust eastward over younger, reddish Triassic rocks to the right or east.

made of silts and sands deposited in the old lake. Talbot Lake, along the road to the northeast of here, is a part of Jasper Lake cut off by drifting sands and the formation of a barrier bar. Edna Lake, much smaller than Talbot, is another part of Jasper Lake cut off by drifting

Jasper Lake is formed in an expanded section of the Athabasca River a few kilometres below Jasper. In fairly recent geological times it was much larger and higher, as is shown by the abandoned terraces and beaches all around its margins.

---

sands. The small dunes and hummocks of wind-blown sand and silt are visible all along the bar separating the two lakes and along the shore of Jasper Lake itself. Near here the drifting sand is right beside the road, and you can see places where it is building up and other places where it is being blown out to leave naked-looking vegetation with its roots exposed.

Several springs issue from the rocks between this stop and the next one at the crossing of the Athabasca River. One of them, called the Cold Sulphur Spring, has a strong SO_2 odour as it gushes out from the base of the roadside cliff. The orifice of the spring is in rocks of lower Devonian age. Fossils of several invertebrate forms occur abundantly in the first half metre or so of limestone directly adjacent to the black shales in the cliffside. The water of the spring itself contains small quantities of sodium chloride (common salt), calcium bicarbonate, magnesium sulphate, and hydrogen sulphide which gives it the smell.

All the springs along here come from surface waters that have penetrated into the rocks, and in their travels through them to the springs, have picked up a variety of substances in solution. Somewhere deep below Cold Sulphur Spring, sulphate-bearing rocks are being chemically altered to provide the smelly SO_2 or rotten-egg gas that is so strong here.

*Roadside stop near dunes to
Athabasca River crossing —
7.7 kilometres (4.8 miles)*

33 Athabasca River Crossing

It is interesting to note that the highway for several kilometres northeast of this crossing is built on the old route of the Grand Trunk Pacific Railway, although road reconstruction in several stages has largely obscured it. In the early part of this century two separate rail lines came up the Athabasca River on opposite sides. With the formation of the Canadian National Railways by the amalgamation of a number of different rail lines in Canada in 1916, different sections of the overlapping railway lines were selected for the main transcontinental line in this area. An abandoned line, from this crossing of the river northeastward, made an ideal site for a highway.

The rocky point on the east bank of the Athabasca River is formed of limestone of the Banff Formation and contains many fossils. Where it is massive, it shows *boiler plates*— smooth, curved, polished surfaces — some of which were scratched by the movement of glacial ice.

To the west of this point (opposite on the right as you look along the road toward Jasper), the three peaks of Chetamon Mountain form an interesting group in which the one on the east or right seems to have a different constitution and appearance from the two to the left. This is because the mountain group is made up of a series of fault slices that dip generally to the west, and along them older rocks have moved up over younger rocks. Thus, the mountain on the right or the east consists of Carboniferous strata. The mountain in the middle of the group consists of the Palliser limestone and older Devonian rocks underneath. The peak on the far left is made of pre-Devonian rocks.

Esplanade Mountain, the next to the right or northeast, consists of Carboniferous rocks on the left slope, Palliser limestone in the peak, and older Devonian rocks in normal sequence down the right flank.

Off to the southwest (a little to the left of straight up the road to Jasper), the great wall of the Palisade is capped by the Palliser limestone, with older rocks in the lower slopes. A distant view of mountains cut in the very old rocks of the central core of the Main Ranges shows through the notch of the Athabasca River valley to the south, with Mount Edith Cavell being the snowy one with layers inclined down and to the right. Northeastward along the Athabasca River valley, the complicated rock mass of Roche Miette stands stark.

Athabasca River crossing to Snaring River bridge area—3.5 kilometres (2.2 miles)

34 Snaring River Bridge Area
The open country in the vicinity of the bridge over the Snaring River provides a wide view in all directions. Directly up the Athabasca River southwest, the great wall of the Palisade is formed of Palliser limestone in the upper parts, a middle slope of shaly facies of older Devonian rocks and a lower cliff of pre-Devonian, possibly Ordovician, strata. From here you may trace the lower cliff of the Palisade across the valley and up the flank of nearby Chetamon Mountain to the peak. The middle peak of Chetamon

Mountain consists of Devonian and Carboniferous rocks and is separated by a fault from the farthest east or right peak, which is made entirely of Mississippian rocks.

Across the Athabasca River a great series of dip-slope mountains in Colin Range extends to the southeast. Morro Peak, at the northwest (or left) end of Colin Range, stands grey above a sharply marked canyon cut by Morro Creek in the Palliser limestone formation. Mount Hawk rises on the south side of the gorge and is capped by the Palliser limestone, with Mississippian rocks on its west slopes. Farther to the right is Mount Colin and below it is the sharply marked gorge of Garonne Creek. Many of the mountains along this edge of Colin Range are excellent examples of sawtooth mountains (see page 40).

The wooded slopes of Signal Mountain to the southeast, and other mountains visible through the gap of the Athabasca River to the south and southeast, belong to the Main Ranges of the Rocky Mountain System. They lie beyond the great fault system that separates their simple structures from the complicated ones of the Front Ranges to the east.

Snaring River bridge to stop at side road to National Parks Training Station—5.0 kilometres (3.1 miles)

The Athabasca River is seen here at the old bridge about twenty kilometres north of Jasper. Behind are the mountains of the Victoria Cross Ranges. The long line of cliffs leads from the Palisade, beyond the left edge of the picture, to the initial slopes of Chetamon Mountain on the right.

35 Roadside Stop at Side Road to National Parks Training Station

Pyramid Mountain stands high to the right, with its snowy back, and the communications tower on its pointed peak. The reddish brown Precambrian sedimentary rocks of Pyramid and its neighbours contrast markedly with the grey limestones of the nearby cliffs of the Palisade. The reason is that the Palisade is at the very edge of the Front Ranges whereas the Pyramid Mountain complex belongs in the Main Ranges of the Rocky Mountains (see page 35). The boundary line is a great fault system that runs for many kilometres to the northwest and southeast. Its trace lies along the wooded flank of Signal Mountain, straight south of here and across the Athabasca River, and separates Maligne Range from the Medicine Lake-Maligne Lake valley and the Front Ranges still farther to the east. Flat-topped terraces, related in origin to the great flooding of the Athabasca River valley in postglacial times (described on page 63) are clearly visible on both sides of the river from this viewpoint. In ditches and road-cuts it may be seen that they are underlain by sands, silts, and well-rounded gravels. The various levels visible are probably the result of the intermittent recession of the lake as the outlet was gradually lowered.

The view northward includes many of the ends of the mountains of the Front Ranges. The valley of Snaring River cuts in close to the foot of the Palisade and separates the Front Ranges from the Main Ranges to the left or southwest. The first complex of peaks to the east or right of the Snaring River valley is Chetamon Mountain. Esplanade Mountain and Mount Greenock are other conspicuous landmarks a little farther to the right in the view.

Directly across the river from this stop, the steeply dipping rocks of Colin Range make a jagged skyline. The tallest peak, with a more or less inverted V-shape and great flat dip surfaces of limestone, is Mount Colin. Immediately to its left and not very distinct is Mount Hawk. Much farther to the left at the end of the range is the rounded profile of Morro Peak. From this viewpoint, part of the very steep walled gorge of Garonne Creek may be seen twisting about beneath Mount Colin. A considerable fan of debris from the cutting of the canyon and the erosion of the terraces is spread out below the lower end of the gorge.

Many of the mountains in this range are clearly of the sawtooth type described on page 40. A spectacular slabby-looking mountain is formed on bare dip slopes of limestone just to the east across the river from here.

Devonian limestones form the

jagged peaks on the skyline, including the tops of Mount Hawk and Mount Colin. The slopes in the foreground, including most of the sawtooth hills and the slightly wooded areas, are in rocks of Mississippian age which overlie the Devonian rocks. As you round the corner going toward Jasper, you can look straight down the road to Mount Edith Cavell 30 kilometres away.

Roadside stop at side road to training station, to roadside stop—
3.5 kilometres (2.2 miles)

Along the highway leading west from Jasper, numerous banks of gravel and sand are exposed with large rounded boulders of a great variety of rocks embedded in them. The high degree of rounding of the boulders shows they have been transported for some distance by running water.

---

36 Roadside Stop

Terraces of the old lake that once filled the valley of the Athabasca River (described on page 63) may be seen clearly on both sides of the valley from this point. Below you the Athabasca is busily cutting and filling, increasing its load in one place and dropping part of it in another. The undercut banks show the former, and the islands in its course are evidence of the latter.

The nearby bank of very round boulders, 15 to 38 centimetres in diameter, in a sandy clay matrix, forms part of one of the terrace deposits dumped in the old flood lake.

Three parallel ridge systems can be seen clearly from this viewpoint. To the northeast and down the Athabasca River valley, the jagged skyline of Colin Range marks the nearest of the Front Ranges of the Rocky Mountain System. To the west, directly opposite the river, the rusty-coloured peak of Pyramid Mountain with its tower, and to the southeast across the river, the lightly wooded hillsides of Signal Mountain form the easternmost part of the Main Ranges of the Rocky Mountain System, which are cut into much more ancient rocks. The third range of mountains is visible far to the south. It is capped by the tilted mass of sedimentary rocks of Mount Edith Cavell. These rocks include the great thickness of Precambrian quartzites and shales of the Pyramid-Signal Range, but they also extend upward into Cambrian quartzites.

Roadside stop to junction with road leading to bridge over the Athabasca River—2.4 kilometres (1.5 miles). End of Roadlog II.

Roadlog III
Jasper to Yellowhead Pass and Mount Robson Area

Start at the junction of Highways 16 and 93 west of Jasper.

Junction to roadside stop beside Miette River—9.3 kilometres (5.8 miles). But read 44 first.

37 Roadside Stop at Picnic Area
In the early days of railroading through the Jasper area, two separate rail lines used the valley of the Miette River and Yellowhead Pass to cross the spine of the Continental Divide. When these lines were amalgamated and the Canadian National Railways formed, overlapping lines were abandoned, and much of the early highway route through this valley was along one of the abandoned railroad beds. You can still see bits of the old right of way here and there, particularly on the left side of the road.

The valley is full of irregular hills of glacial debris, and large boulders abound. Bedrock is quartzite, pebble conglomerate, argillite, and slate of Precambrian age with abundant quartz veins making white streaks in some outcrops. A long outcrop of these old rocks is in the rock-cut about a kilometre down the road, and the rocks there are pretty well typical of what you will encounter all the way to Yellowhead Pass and the boundary of the park.

The Whistlers and Muhigan Mountain lie just to the south of the road but are rarely visible because the road follows along their lower slopes and they are obscured by woods and intervening shoulders. The high hills and snowy peaks, that begin to show in the distance through the valley gap soon after you start out, are those of Yellowhead Mountain on the Continental Divide.

The roadside stop is a pleasant place to see the Miette River in its beds of sand and gravel, not very effective as an agent of erosion at this stage of geological history and almost certainly occupying a valley which was carved by larger rivers and glaciers before the present stream came to occupy it.

Roadside stop to bridge over Clairvaux Creek—6.4 kilometres (4.0 miles)

38 Roadside Stop at Bridge over Clairvaux Creek

The mountains along here are all cut into Precambrian rocks with some possibly of lower Cambrian age here and there. Upstream and to the left, you can see that Clairvaux Creek has cut a sharp-walled canyon in the hillside, contrasting with the open, flat-bottomed valley of Miette River below. The canyon is being cut by the stream occupying it in an early

stage of development whereas the open valley was cut some time ago, then filled with glacial deposits, and the present stream wanders around on the flat without much real relationship to the valley it now occupies. The pattern of the glacial deposits and the shape of the country generally suggest that a major tributary glacier poured into the Athabasca Valley from the Miette Valley.

Rock outcrops are the same quartzites, argillites, slates of some variety, and pebbly conglomerates with numerous white quartz veins seen all along this route. The high, snowy peaks that become more and more prominent in the valley gap to the west along the road are part of the Yellowhead Mountain complex on the Continental Divide.

About one and a half kilometres beyond Clairvaux Creek the road has a large rock-cut along the left side and falls away to a meadowy open valley below. It would make a good stopping place but such cuts are sometimes dangerous because of occasional rockfalls, so we may note what is to be seen in passing. The rock in the artificial cliffs is a heavy slate with slaty cleavage almost exactly parallel to the layering of the original beds. Below, the Miette River, really only a large brook along here, wanders around on the valley flat of glacial gravels filling the valley to a depth of many tens of metres. Scars of the old road are on the opposite side of the valley and show that glacial deposits are only thinly overlaid here and there on the valley wall.

Beyond the end of the visible road is a series of high, snowy ridges from Caledonia Peak on the right to the various peaks of Yellowhead Mountain disappearing behind the wooded ridge to the left. The bold peaks of Mount Bridgeland, at over 2,804 metres (9,200 feet) to the right are a little mindful of Mount Eisenhower in Banff National Park. From the Jasper end of this hill and cut, you can see the rocky top of Mount Tekarra, about opposite Mount Edith Cavell in the Athabasca Valley, a few kilometres south of Jasper.

Clairvaux Creek to summit of Yellowhead Pass and park boundary—9.3 kilometres (5.8 miles)

39 Summit of Yellowhead Pass and Park Boundary

One of the lowest places on the Continental Divide is at Yellowhead Pass, only 1,131 metres (3,711 feet) above sea level. Water flows eastward from this divide through

Mumm Peak is a mass of Precambrian and Cambrian quartzite and limestone in the northwestern section of the park. In this view, across the valley of the Smoky River, a cirque can be seen clearly on the side of the peak.

The lower valley of Mural Glacier shows the conical remnants of glacial debris once plastered along its sides.

Miette River to join the Athabasca River near Jasper and finally empty into the Arctic Ocean. Water flows westward into a tributary of the Fraser River and ends ultimately in the Pacific Ocean at Vancouver. The divide here is part of the Alberta-British Columbia boundary and is the western boundary of Jasper National Park.

Farther along, this road provides access to the Mount Robson area some 65 kilometres to the west. Mount Robson, the highest point in the Canadian Rockies at 3,954 metres (12,972 feet) above sea level, lies just to the west of the Continental Divide and, therefore, just out of Jasper National Park. An extensive tract has been set aside along this side of the Continental Divide as Mount Robson Provincial Park. Entry to the northwestern parts of Jasper National Park is via

trail to Mount Robson and Berg Lake, thence through Robson Pass to the headwaters of Smoky River.

Mural Glacier covers a gently sloping area down Mumm Peak, but near its foot it tumbles over a great cliff.

40 Northwest Corner of Jasper National Park via Trail to Mount Robson and Berg Lake

The northwest corner of the park is generally inaccessible except by horse and foot trails. The most spectacular and most travelled of these trails leaves the highway and the railway opposite Mount Robson station, passes up the Robson River through deep woods to Kinney Lake, thence over flat river deposits to the beginning of a series of great steps over which the Robson River makes several spectacular falls, and on to the flat country around Berg Lake. This route starts opposite the southwestern face of Mount Robson and goes around the western end to the northwest and northern

129

slopes. Berg Lake receives glacial ice and meltwater from the slopes all along the north side of the Mount Robson complex.

The trail continues beyond Berg Lake over an area of alluvial deposits to Robson Pass on the boundary between Mount Robson and Jasper parks. It is interesting to note that when the boundary was established, Robson Glacier extended farther down the valley than it does now. Its meltwaters at that time spread both westward and eastward onto both sides of the Continental Divide. Nowadays only a very small trickle of water from rain and melting snow passes into the brooks draining to the northeast, but the boundary remains as it was originally laid out.

Adolphus Lake lies at the very head of the Smoky River, whose drainage basin makes the northwestern part of Jasper National Park. Its waters drain northward and leave the park along its northern boundary, near which they are joined by the drainage from Twintree Creek and Lake. From the Adolphus Lake area, the scenery to the northwest is dominated by Mumm Peak whose northwestern slopes contain the snowfields that give rise to Mural Glacier.

The whole northwestern section of Jasper National Park, along with the Mount Robson area in Mount Robson Provincial Park, is a very spectacular part of the Rocky Mountain scenery, and a trip into the area is very rewarding for the traveller.

To the east of the Smoky River and Twintree Creek drainage basins, rivers lead eastward and southeastward into the Snake Indian River drainage system which occupies a very large portion of the northern section of Jasper National Park. Riding and walking trails follow the main river system throughout this primitive and beautiful mountain area.

Opposite: The main route into the northwest corner of Jasper National Park passes up the valley of the Robson River to Berg Lake at the foot of Mount Robson. This view of the highest peak in the Canadian Rockies is from the shoulder of Mumm Peak, on the boundary between Jasper National Park and Mount Robson Provincial Park.

Several unusual drainage features mark the valleys of Maligne River and its tributaries. This lake, about two kilometres east of the Medicine Lake and Maligne Lake road, has a rushing white brook coming into its far end, yet no visible outlet. Its waters join a vast underground drainage system.

Roadlog IV
Jasper to Maligne Lake
Area

Centre of Jasper at CN station
northeastward to road junction and
bridge over Athabasca River—about
4.0 kilometres (2.5 miles)

41

Turn across the bridge, and at the junction just beyond, follow the signs to Edith Lake along the branch road. In this area, the sandy flat was once the bottom of a lake that filled the whole Athabasca River valley for many kilometres above and below here. Meltwater streams brought vast quantities of sand and silt into the ancient lake where they spread over the irregular glacial deposits already there. As the level of the old lake gradually went down with the cutting away or melting of the dam at its lower end, irregular depressions in the various deposits in the bottom of the valley stayed filled with water to form the system of lakes that we now know as Edith, Annette, Beauvert and other smaller ones.

The very beautiful colour of these lakes may be due to one or a combination of several factors. Very finely divided sediment suspended in glacial meltwaters and the streams that come from them com-

monly gives a pale green or turquoise colour to water when the coarser particles have settled out. Large quantities of calcium carbonate or limestone in solution also tend to impart this colour to water. In many lakes the colour of the water is greatly intensified if the bottom is made of light-coloured muds or silts. In some of the lakes in this district, very fine-grained white sediments on the bottom intensify the blue-green colour already inherent in the water.

Road junction of Highway 16 and
Maligne Lake road to first overlook—
about 6.4 kilometres (4.0 miles)

42 Stop at First Overlook

After sweeping up the hillside in gentle curves, the road flattens a little and a parking lot and extensive overlook are on the left. A very short distance beyond is a bridge over the Maligne River with a tea room, parking lot, and another set of walks and viewpoints to the left. The two areas will be treated separately, with the general view in the first and the Maligne Canyon in the second.

The first overlook provides a superb view out over the whole Athabasca Valley. Picture it full of ice as a great glacier, drawing its sustenance from the surrounding mountains, pushed eastward (right). As it melted, great quantities of boulders, sand, and fine silt poured off its sides in meltwaters and these are now seen in the pale yellowish banks and terraces. The flat tops on some of them are because they were made in temporary lakes, often between the main ice in the valley and the hills on the sides. Places that were not filled in or that were occupied by remnants of the waning ice after the rest had gone are now the hollows filled with water and called the Jasper Lake, Edna Lake, and Antoinette Lake. In summer they are turquoise.

From here, the rusty dark red mass of Pyramid Mountain, with its tiny communications tower on its peak and wooded lower slopes, looms in the sky across the valley. To its right the grey limestone of the Palisade angles up to the right. Between these two masses a great fault has brought the older Pyramid rocks high above the younger limestones. The same fault separates Signal Mountain, the mostly wooded one to the far left as you face out over the valley, from the younger rocks exposed in the canyon below this lookout and the limestone peaks back and to the right in the Colin Range. Long lines of mountains with some snow patches beyond Jasper town lie on each side of the Miette River valley, the route of the Yellowhead highway to the west.

You may note the mixture of stones in the wall around this view-point. They are a great mixture of pink, yellow, and grey quartzites from the older rock formations with occasional dark blocks of limestone from the younger groups. You may note, too, that a lot of them are split round boulders, the rounding proving that they have been water-rolled some time in their history. Below rumbles the Maligne River with an interesting story of its own to be seen in the next several stops.

Just beyond this stop is another parking area where you can walk to several places to observe the Maligne River. At the bridge and beside the tea room, it flows on top of the surface of the bedrock and between banks of glacial debris. Just below the bridge it begins to cut down in the massive grey Palliser limestone along bedding planes that dip gently to the west. Within a few metres it starts cutting vertically into the limestones, and in about a kilometre descends almost 150 metres toward the general level of the valley floor of the Athabasca River. Its steep-sided canyon is as much as 60 metres deep with adjacent walls only a few metres apart. In some of the narrowest places, boulders and blocks of rocks are jammed between the walls part way down.

The canyon has been cut by a combination of solution and abrasion, as may be seen in the remnants of potholes within the walls of the canyon and in the apparent control of its course along joint planes in the Palliser limestone. The canyon has come from gradual erosion headward by the swift-flowing Maligne River from an original waterfall that must have formed on a cliff on the side of the main Athabasca River valley in post-glacial time.

You will soon realize that there is something very strange about this gorge which starts out with such a small brook in it and within a few hundred metres is a full-fledged river. A complete description of why this is and what is happening starts on page 42.

Maligne River crossing and Maligne Canyon tea room stop to bridge crossing Two Valley Creek — 4.8 kilometres (3.0 miles)

43 Bridge Crossing Two Valley Creek

The road along the valley of the Maligne River below Medicine Lake is cut principally in the limestones of the Palliser Formation. This is natural because the valley would be expected to follow the general strike of the rock structures in the area.

The bridge over the creek affords a view of another of the many steep-walled gorges cut into the limestones of these mountains. You can see from its shape that the gorge has been cut by a combination of abrasion or wearing away by mechanical action, and solution, which produces rounded surfaces. Remnants of potholes are visible in some places. The bottom of the canyon is perpetually gloomy, with the constant rumbling of falling water. To the left, forests and smaller vegetation cling to the grey dip slopes of the limestone beds. Along here you get occasional glimpses of the spires of the Colin Range marching off into the distance.

Bridge over Two Valley Creek to northwest end of Medicine Lake — 10.3 kilometres (6.4 miles)

44 Northwest End of Medicine Lake

As you drive the last kilometre or two to the end of Medicine Lake, you may notice that the Maligne River to your right disappears almost completely. During most of the year, a walk around the end of Medicine Lake will show that there is no outlet at all. For a brief period in the middle and late summer, Medicine Lake spills out over the rocky channelway so that there is a thread of water all the way down. At other times, however, it drains by underground channels. Indeed, in the late fall the lake bottom is mostly bare with the Maligne River entering its upper end, wandering over the flats and then disappearing down holes as described on page 42.

The whole northeast side of Medicine Lake is dominated by the great dip slopes of grey limestone with talus and rubble heaps at their feet. Boulders, which have come from the erosion of the cliffs above, line the northeast shore of Medicine Lake. Along the southwest side of the lake two gorges cut in limestones mark the courses of brooks that have spewed out their debris in the form of fans at lake level. Remnants of flat gravel terraces are visible in a few places along the shore, showing that the level of Medicine Lake was at one time higher than it is now.

Northwest end of Medicine Lake to southeast end— 7.8 kilometres (4.9 miles)

45 Southeast End of Medicine Lake

The view northward from the southeast end of Medicine Lake shows two ranges of mountains cut in steeply tilted limestones and shales. The ridge closest to the northeast shore shows great dip slopes of grey limestone with partly wooded scree and talus heaps. To the right, a sharply marked valley leads into the Beaver Lake area. A second series of spectacular sawtooth ridges is visible from the end of the lake, with the massive grey limestones holding up the main ridge and overlying brownish shales

and minor limestones in the sawtooth spurs. Here is where you see the great gush of the Maligne River pouring with Medicine Lake in summer, with no equivalent out-flow.

Southeast end of Medicine Lake to northwest end of Maligne Lake— 16.1 kilometres (10.0 miles)

46 Northwest End of Maligne Lake

The road between the southeast end of Medicine Lake and the northwest end of Maligne Lake follows a valley that was heavily glaciated in the recent geological past. As the ice melted and retreated from this valley, large deposits of glacial debris were dumped all along it. The Maligne River, which drops more than 210 metres in 11 kilometres, flows swiftly along in a course choked with gravel and great boulders left by the ice long ago.

Maligne Lake itself is the result of the deepening of the upper end of the valley by the glaciers and the damming of the valley by sand, gravel, and rock rubble in the vicinity of its present northwest end. Depressions called *kettles* are numerous in the woods beside the road in the last kilometre or so before the boathouses and tea rooms at the northwest end of Maligne Lake. They originated when parts of the glaciers became

Eight kilometres east of the upper end of Medicine Lake, rugged mountains hem in this beautiful little tarn, a small lake formed in a glacially carved bowl. The brook in the right foreground drains into the Rocky River.

Above: In summer the melting snows raise the level of Maligne River between Maligne Lake and Medicine Lake so that it becomes this rushing torrent.
Below: The view northward from the southeast end of Medicine Lake shows a series of spectacular ridges of Devonian limestone standing nearly up on edge.

isolated during melting and then were covered deeply in sand and gravel by the outwashing meltwaters. The isolated blocks of ice gradually melted, causing the overlying sands and gravels to sag and make the hollows. Some of these kettles are dry; others hold small ponds.

The view to the southeast down Maligne Lake is very beautiful indeed. Wooded slopes to the right or south lead gradually upward to the rounded lower slopes of mountains belonging to the Main Ranges of the Rocky Mountain System. The great boundary fault between the Front Ranges to the east and the Main Ranges to the west, in this neighbourhood passes along the slope of the hills 3 to 4 kilometres inland from the southwestern shores of Maligne Lake.

A group of great peaks far down the lake to the right includes Mount Unwin and Mount Charlton, both more than 3,200 metres (10,500 feet) above sea level, and others which are only partly visible behind them. This block of mountains belongs to the Front Ranges. On the left or northeast side of the lake the peaks, generally not snow-covered, include Leah Peak, the nearest; Samson Peak next farther down; and a complex of other mountains described at stops 47 and 48.

Northwest end of Maligne Lake to the Narrows—14.2 kilometres (8.8 miles)

47   Narrows of Maligne Lake

It is the fate of all lakes to be but temporary features of the scenery. The outlets are constantly cutting down so that they will be drained eventually. Brooks which come into them feed a load of sediments to fill them in gradually. At the middle section of Maligne Lake a river coming in from the east has built a very considerable delta of sand, silt, and rock rubble from the nearby mountains. This has nearly cut the lake in two at a place that was probably somewhat restricted anyway by a pile of glacial debris. It is predictable that the delta of the stream will gradually extend outward to make two lakes out of the one long one that is here now.

Visitors to this area will recognize the view from the southeast end of the narrows as one of the best known in the Rocky Mountains. At one spot, where touring boats usually stop, a small rise supports a number of tall trees. At times this rise is surrounded by water to form an island, while at others it is connected to the adjacent point by a small isthmus. A commonly seen and very beautiful picture is one that may be taken from the bank just behind this island.

Mount Paul is the great mountain to the left with the spiky peak and the great limestone cliffs with the talus slopes below. Mounts Monkhead and Warren continue the line of snow-covered mountains to the southeast. Farther to the right, Mount Mary Vaux and Llysyfran Peak form a great rock wall with glaciers feeding into meltwater streams in the valleys below. Wooded deltas, which are gradually growing out into the lake as the streams continue to pour sediments into the upper end, are to be seen in three places toward the southeastern tip.

Narrows to southeastern end of Maligne Lake— 7.1 kilometres (4.4 miles)

48 Southeastern End of Maligne Lake

The great walls of Cambrian limestone in the mountains all around remind us that these are sedimentary rocks laid down in ancient seas that covered this area hundreds of millions of years ago. Mountains were then made from the ancient sediments by folding, faulting and uplift, followed by lengthy erosion. They form part of a great chain of mountains that extends for thousands of kilometres along the western rib of North America from the Arctic Ocean to Panama. Most of the major features of the mountains were carved by river erosion over the millions of years following their uplift. A sharpening of the topography and formation of most of the great cliffs were the result of glaciation of the region in comparatively recent geological times. The formation of talus slopes at the foot of the cliffs and a small amount of local glacial cutting have modified the scenery a little since the main glaciers left.

Look again at the great walls of rock on each side and think of the fine particles of silt and limy mud settling on the bottom of the ocean so long ago, and the enormous amount of time it must have taken for this mass of rocks to form even before the beginning of uplift and the carving of the mountains began.

Roadlog V
From Jasper along
Southwest Side of
Athabasca River to
Athabasca Falls Junction,
with a Side Trip to Mount
Edith Cavell.

Proceed south from Jasper to the junction of Routes 93 and 16.

Jasper junction south along 93 to junction 93A — 6.1 kilometres (3.8 miles)

Along 93A from junction to turnoff to Marmot Basin — 2.4 kilometres (1.5 miles)

49

In climbing up the hillside on Route 93A, the old main road to Banff, one can see out over the valley of the Athabasca River in a great sweeping view. This·extends from the downfold of Mount Kerkeslin, up the valley to the southeast, past the castlelike rocky top of Mount Tekarra about opposite, past the view down the Athabasca Valley that extends all the way out to the plains, to the dark mass behind Jasper dominated by Pyramid Mountain. Away below, the river traverses its valley with islands and cut-banks scattered along its course.

The road to Marmot Basin winds up the hillside to the right but affords little more than an elaboration of the view from along the road on the way up here, except that there are one or two places where you can see directly into Mount Edith Cavell; and where it crosses Portal Creek, sharp pointed Mount Peven dominates the valley up which goes the trail into the Tonquin country. Everywhere along this side road, and indeed along 93A, banks of glacial debris are of considerable thickness.

From Marmot Basin turnoff to junction with road to Mount Edith Cavell — 2.7 kilometres (1.7 miles)

From junction with 93A along Mount Edith Cavell side road to viewpoint — 3.7 kilometres (2.3 miles)

50   Viewpoint on Right (West) Side of Road
This stop provides a view of the valley of the rushing Astoria River with its green and white water. Far to the north, the dark reddish grey mass of Pyramid Mountain dominates the skyline beyond Jasper. A little to the right is the vast sweep of the valley of Athabasca River with distant mountain ranges to the north. Southward up the valley looms the mass of Mount Edith Cavell.

At and across from this view-

Right: About halfway along the branch road to Mount Edith Cavell, this view of the steep-walled valley of the Astoria River shows the flanks of the valley covered with glacial debris. Erosion of the lightly cemented sand, clay and boulders has produced the patterns on the far wall and the spiky pinnacles in the foreground.

Below: From the peak of Aquila Mountain, Mount Edith Cavell is seen to be part of a vast mass of rock that dips gently westward.

point, a great plug of glacial deposits has been cut through by the Astoria River. The boulders in the deposits are slightly rounded and a faint banding can be seen in the cliff opposite, suggesting that these are water-worn deposits, perhaps laid down in meltwaters in front of or beside a tongue of ice that once occupied the Astoria River valley. When dry, this mixture of boulders, sand, and clay seems fairly strong, but when wet it is probably soft and almost fluid so that land slips are frequent, as shown in the bank on the other side of the river. The material is eroded rapidly and irregularly so that some pillars are left, as in the cliff immediately below the viewpoint. It does not seem to have the right consistency to make the tall *hoodoos* which are found in Yoho National Park and, less well developed, in Banff National Park.

Viewpoint on right (west) side of road
to summit viewpoint on right (west)
side of road—8.5 kilometres
(5.3 miles)

51 Summit Viewpoint on Right or West Side of Road

The road to Mount Edith Cavell here swings more and more southwesterly away from the Astoria River valley. To the south, Mount Edith Cavell thrusts its series of layers of rocks and snow into the sky. Its nearer right shoulder is made of dark reddish quartzites which contrast with the dark green forests at its base.

Westward, the gently curved Astoria River valley stretches off to the snow-covered mountains on the Continental Divide. On the distant skyline a part of Fraser Glacier gleams white, with Bennington Peak on its right and the mighty Ramparts around the corner just out of sight. On the right or the north side of the Astoria River valley, Oldhorn Mountain shows layers of left or inward dipping quartzite. Immediately opposite the viewpoint is Franchère Peak with reddish and brownish weathering quartzite with a southerly dip.

On the left side of the Astoria River valley, beyond the rusty right-hand mass of Edith Cavell, is Throne Mountain, so aptly called because of the great amphitheatre or thronelike basin carved in its near face. This is a cirque that has been made by ancient glaciers.

From this viewpoint you may also notice the scree slopes below the major mountains, snowslide areas that cut swaths through the heavy forest, and occasional glimpses of the Astoria River with its islands, gravel bars and cut banks, and its constant roar.

Summit viewpoint to Mount Edith
Cavell—2.1 kilometres (1.3 miles)

52 Mount Edith Cavell

This area is described on pages 57 to 60.

From the parking lot at the end of the road, you can walk up the paths on either side of the valley or pick your way over the rock rubble in the valley bottom itself. This is an ideal place to see *lateral moraines,* the steep-walled deposits of debris left along the sides of glaciers. Here, too, you can see Angel Glacier, left hanging on the cliff by a gradual retreat of the ice, the magnificent cliffs on the inside face of Mount Edith Cavell, the runnels and erosion channels in the snow patches high on the flanks of the mountain, faceted and *striated* (scratched) boulders, and a great variety of other features of glaciers and their deposits.

It is interesting to note that a small lake has formed in front of the melting ice in the centre of the amphitheatre formed by the lateral moraines and the cliffs of Mount Edith Cavell, at a point about opposite the end of Angel Glacier. If melting continues to exceed the addition of ice at the back, the lake will get larger and larger.

On very calm days in this mammoth rock bowl, the distant sound of running water and the occasional crash of ice or rock waste from the glacier or the mountainsides add to the feeling of hugeness of the surroundings.

The glacial deposits just uphill from the parking lot are covered with mosses and small trees. This shows that the glaciers retreated from this area at least several tens of years ago.

It is well worth a walk a few hundred metres down the beginning of the Tonquin Valley trail which leaves the main road about a kilometre from the parking lot. The view from the footbridge over the brook that drains tiny Cavell Lake is one of the most beautiful in the Rocky Mountains.

From Mount Edith Cavell back to junction with Highway 93A —
14.5 kilometres (9.0 miles)

Mount Edith Cavell junction to stop beside Athabasca River —
5.0 kilometres (3.1 miles)

53 Stop beside the Athabasca River

At this point you are nearly at the level of the Athabasca River as it rushes by with its grey silt-laden waters, cutting, carrying, depositing on its way to the sea. Straight down the road (southward toward Banff) the tower of Brussels Peak leads to the peak of Mount Christie to the left. The downfold or syncline of Mount Kerkeslin shows old rusty quartzites and has Mount Hardisty, without much form, on its left with brownish scree slopes and snow patches. Across the valley and along

Above: The road to Mount Edith Cavell runs along the valley of Astoria River. On the left is Throne Mountain at 3,092 metres (10,144 feet) and at right is Oldhorn Mountain at 2,981 metres (9,779 feet). The southern extension of the Ramparts is seen in the distance. *Below:* The main depression below Angel Glacier on Mount Edith Cavell is littered with rock waste from earlier glaciers.

The mighty Ramparts loom moodily above Amethyst Lakes on a cloudy July day. The rubble at their foot has been modified by snow and glacial ice into ridges and terminal moraines.

it to the left, the gently sloped and wooded ridge leads to Tekarra's cliffs and then to the rounded slopes of Signal Mountain on the end of the ridge. Partly in the trees is Pyramid Mountain more or less straight up the road toward Jasper.

In the short time it has taken you to read this paragraph, hundreds of cubic metres of melted ice and snow have rushed past this spot; and several tonnes of sediment, the waste of the eroding mountains, have passed on their way to their ultimate deposition in the faraway sea.

Stop beside Athabasca River to north or near end of Leech Lake— 9.2 kilometres (5.7 miles)

54 Leech Lake Stop

The mass of Whirlpool Mountain

looms above the far end of Leech Lake and has a snowy top with long runnels down its flanks. To the left, various peaks culminate in the synclinal top of younger, yellowish-grey dolomites of Mount Fryatt. To those accustomed to the usual pictures of Mount Edith Cavell, it is a surprise to realize that the plateau to the right is the mass supporting the central peak of Edith Cavell in a sort of back view. When you round the next corner, there is Mount Christie to the left with the rock layer sloping

Seen here from Thunderbolt Peak, Mount Edith Cavell is the white peak in the centre distance, framed between Throne Mountain on the left and Blackhorn Mountain on the right.

down to the right and the great funnellike mass of Brussels Peak sitting in the saddle.

Leech Lake stop to Athabasca Falls — 4.4 kilometres (2.7 miles) and to junction of 93 and 93A — 4.7 kilometres (2.9 miles) (see Stop 14, page 98).

147

One of the superb views in walking distance of Jasper is from the top of the Palisade. In this view, looking northwest across Jasper Lake, a small part of the great plains can be seen on the skyline through the notch framed by angular Roche Miette on the right and Bedson Ridge on the left.

Roadlog VI
Excursion from Jasper to
Palisade Lookout Tower

55

A road leads north from Jasper to Patricia Lake and to Pyramid Lake beyond it. From the end of the road at the outlet of Pyramid Lake, a woods road leads to the lookout tower on top of the Palisade. On a clear day this lookout point provides a superb view of the Rocky Mountains and is well worth an all-day excursion for those willing to walk.

From Pyramid Lake itself there is a good view of Pyramid Mountain, which rears its reddish brown head to an elevation of 2,766 metres (9,076 feet) above sea level. It is made of red and orange lower Cambrian quartzites and Precambrian quartzites and argillites which dip gently eastward. This means that older rocks lie to the left in the flanks of Pyramid Mountain and its subsidiary, Cairngorm Mountain, and younger rocks lie to the right.

From parts of the road along Pyramid Lake, a view nearly due west shows a number of quite high mountains near the Continental Divide and the western boundary of Jasper National Park.

The woods road leads upward along the inside slope of the Palisade from the end of the road on Pyramid Lake, where cars may be parked, to the lookout tower. A number of branch trails go eastward to the edge of the Palisade, if you do not want to go all the way to the top.

The view from the lookout tower shows a magnificent panorama of jagged mountain peaks stretching away to the east in row upon row. These are the Front Ranges of the Rocky Mountain System. They consist of a series of fault blocks which have been thrust up, one over the next adjacent one (see page 35).

The Athabasca River may be seen from a point many kilometres above Jasper to well beyond the end of Jasper Lake, 25 kilometres to the east. Snaring River comes down its wooded valley from the northwest to mingle its darker waters with the silt-laden Athabasca River below the railway bridge.

Opposite you, steeply dipping Devonian rocks make jagged peaks along Colin Range, with V-wedges of Carboniferous rocks on their near slopes. Morro Peak at the northwest end of Colin Range is separated from the other peaks by a very narrow, deep canyon cut across the rock formations by Morro Creek. Farther to the right, below the great slabs of limestone in the tallest peak (Mount Colin, 2,687 metres or 8,815 feet), another deep canyon (Garonne Creek) cuts across the trend of the rocks. An array of dip slopes, inverted V's on sawtooth ridges, and sweeping lines of individual outcropping sedimentary rocks are presented all along the front of the mountains.

The distant view down the Athabasca River valley shows the ridges of the Front Ranges one after another; the flatter country to the east of the Rockies shows in the gap made by the valley in the farthest mountains. Conspicuous to the right of Jasper Lake is the abrupt front of Roche Miette, made by a cliff of the Palliser limestone. The terraces of the great lake that filled this valley for 95 kilometres in postglacial times may be seen along the valley sides, particularly to the left of the main bend of the river opposite Morro Peak.

The rock at the lookout tower is the Palliser limestone that forms the great cliff immediately in front of and below you. Just across the small depression to the west is a brownish bank of shaly rocks of the Banff Formation in which fossils of ancient marine creatures are fairly abundant. The much older Pyramid quartzites stick up over it farther west. It is interesting to note that the great fault separating the Main Ranges of the Rocky Mountains on the west from the Front Ranges to the east, lies between the near brown ridge and Pyramid Mountain. This fault surface separates not only two structural units of different kinds but also separates fossiliferous rocks from rocks formed long before the origin of life in the form we know it.

56 Trail to Tonquin Valley

A horse and walking trail to Tonquin Valley leaves the Mount Edith Cavell road about two and a half kilometres north of the chalet. Just below the main road, Cavell Lake forms a perfect reflecting pool for Mount Edith Cavell, and this spot provides one of the most beautiful sights in all the Canadian Rockies.

The trail follows westward along the south side of the Astoria River for about 5 kilometres. To the south, the great bulk of Edith Cavell is succeeded westward by the mass of Throne Mountain. Northward the peaks, some of them very sharp, are all between 2,750 and 3,050 metres (9,000 and 10,000 feet) above sea level. They include Franchère, the farthest east, and Oldhorn, the farthest west. The Astoria River itself is a fast-flowing, green-watered brook which takes the drainage from many glaciers along the Continental Divide and from the Amethyst Lakes in the main Tonquin Valley itself. All the rocks along the Astoria River valley are Precambrian.

57 Tonquin Valley

Tonquin Valley is an area of gently rolling country between a mass of mountains to the east and the mighty wall of rock, called the Ramparts, along the Continental Divide to the west. Open alpine meadows are common on the east side and the north end. The Amethyst Lakes, formed by the damming of the valley system by glacial deposits, are very beautiful in their setting against the irregular cliffs and peaks of the Ramparts. All the mountains in the view from here are carved in Precambrian rocks and most are in quartzite — ancient sands which have been consolidated and somewhat recrystallized to form this tough dense rock.

South of the Amethyst Lakes, an area of very high mountains with numerous valley glaciers provides spectacular scenery. Mount Erebus, about 5 kilometres due south of the Amethyst Lakes, reaches 3,120 metres (10,234 feet) above sea level. In the Ramparts themselves, Mount Bennington, at 3,270 metres (10,726 feet), forms a corner on the Continental Divide where the boundary swings more westward from its southeasterly and southward course in front of the Amethyst Lakes.

Another route is via trails that leave the Marmot Basin side road at its crossing of Portal Creek. Steep-sided Peven Peak dominates the view up the departure valley and the trail passes left or south of this mass of Precambrian rock, through the Portal and Maccarib Pass out into the open Tonquin Valley.

Those going into Tonquin Valley will note that its superb mountain scenery is of the kind seen again and again in parts of Jasper National Park away from the main highways.

Green glacial streams sing in their new found freedom,
After aeons of waiting and slow, plastic twistings and turnings
In the valley depths
To emerge at the glacier's foot into the
Wakening touch of the warm summer sun.

David Baird

Epilogue

On foot, on horseback, by car or by train—however you travel in Jasper National Park, you will be impressed by the sheer beauty and magnificence of your surroundings. The feeling of delight brought to the senses by the mountains and streams, the forests and the snows, is matched by the feeling of awe brought by a knowledge of the long geological history behind each part of the landscape. Lofty mountains covered with snow and ice stand now where once the waves of ancient seas moved in rhythmic procession. Valleys now filled with beautiful forests and rushing streams were once occupied by great glaciers that ground slowly forward, pushing all before them. Steep-walled chasms now echo the sounds of falling water of streams which once flowed at higher levels but have slowly cut their way down through the solid rocks. Lakes that now sparkle in the summer sun lie in bowls carved by moving ice long ago.

We are fortunate indeed that such large areas of this beautiful country have been set aside for the enjoyment of all who come their way.

Index

For more information on the geology of Jasper National Park see the following publications.

A Guide to Geology for Visitors in Canada's National Parks, by D.M. Baird. Published by Macmillan Co., Toronto. Also available from the Publishing Centre, Supply and Services Canada, Ottawa K1A 0S9, or from any of the national parks. This pocket-size book describes the general principles of geology with special references to the national parks of Canada, written in layman's language (about 160 pages, 50 illustrations).

Mount Robson (Southeast) Map-area, by E. W. Mountjoy, Geological Survey of Canada, Paper 61-31. Describes in detail the geology of most of the northern part of Jasper National Park, with maps and diagrams. Although written for the professional geologist, it contains information of interest to the traveller.

Alberta Society of Petroleum Geologists—Guidebook for the 5th Annual Field Conference, Jasper National Park, 1955. A professional approach to the geology of Jasper National Park. This book includes general articles on the history of the Jasper area, details of the geology in certain areas, and roadlogs for certain highways. Available from the Alberta Society of Petroleum Geologists, 631 8th Ave. W., Calgary, Alberta.

Geology and Economic Minerals of Canada. Economic Geology Series No. 1 (1957) of the Geological Survey of Canada. This compilation of the geology of all of Canada contains a great deal of information on the western mountains. Available from the Publishing Centre, Ottawa, or from the Geological Survey of Canada, Ottawa.

Particular questions of a geological nature concerning Jasper National Park should be addressed to the Geological Survey of Canada, Ottawa, or to the office of the Geological Survey in Calgary or Vancouver.

For information on all other matters concerning the park, write to Parks Canada Information Division, Ottawa K1A 0H4.